99 things to do
BETWEEN **HERE** AND **HEAVEN**

99

BETWEEN

KATHLEEN LONG BOSTROM
and PETER GRAYSTONE

things
to do

HERE AND **HEAVEN**

WJK WESTMINSTER
JOHN KNOX PRESS
LOUISVILLE • KENTUCKY

1st edition
Published by Westminster John Knox Press
Louisville, Kentucky

09 10 11 12 13 14 15 16 17 18—10 9 8 7 6 5 4 3 2 1

Book design by Drew Stevens
Cover art: © DMH Images/Getty Images
Cover design by designpointinc.com

Library of Congress Cataloging-in-Publication Data

Bostrom, Kathleen Long.
  99 things to do between here and heaven / Kathleen Long Bostrom and
Peter Graystone. — 1st ed.
    p. cm.
  ISBN 978-0-664-23324-2 (alk. paper)
  1. Self-actualization (Psychology)—Religious aspects—Christianity.
I. Graystone, Peter. II. Title. III. Title: Ninety-nine things to do
between here and heaven.
  BV4598.2.B67 2009
  248.4'6—dc22

                                                        2009006819

Introduction

You're going to love this book!

From the first entry to the last, *99 Things to Do between Here and Heaven* is full of brilliant ideas for enriching your life. The format is reader friendly. Each entry provides the basic information that you'll need, reactions you might expect to experience, appropriate quotes, and Bible passages that all tie together. There's a space where you can record your accomplishments, and there are prompts that encourage you to ponder how the experiences have affected your life. The author's wit and humor enhance the creative challenges that are presented. The overall result is a book that is a celebration of life and is guaranteed to nourish your spirit.

Yes, this is a great book. I wish I'd written it!

My job as writer has been to edit the insightful material written by Peter Graystone. I've combed through the pages and made changes that adapt the book to a North American audience; changed the spelling of certain words ("flavour" to "flavor"); revised Web site addresses; and tweaked what I consider to be charming "British-isms" (in the United States, we use "Zip codes" rather than "postcodes" [#19] and "elevators" instead of "lifts" [#7]). In some cases, an original entry has been rewritten—again, for the purpose of suiting the readership of this version.

I am grateful to have had the opportunity to edit Peter Graystone's gem of a book. Not only am I now inspired to experience as many of the suggestions as I can, I've thought of a few of my own. Once you've completed the ninety-nine ideas revealed here, why not add a few of your own?

Enjoy the journey! Every day of life is a gift.

Kathleen Long Bostrom
April 2009

Contents

Here are all 99 things to do between here and Heaven.
Check the star as you achieve each one. If a friend or
relative has done it too, write their name next to it.

v	Introduction	
1	Watch the sun rise	
2	Bake bread	
3	Read a Gospel in one sitting	
4	Give blood	
5	Examine an icon	
6	Give your testimony	
7	Learn a musical instrument	
8	Learn about Judaism	
9	Help fight poverty through microfinance	
10	Go on a protest rally	
11	Revisit your childhood self	
12	Take part in a Tenebrae service	
13	Bury a time capsule	
14	Break a bad habit	
15	Learn about New Testament Greek	
16	Milk a cow	
17	Light a candle	
18	Go on a retreat	
19	Make a will	
20	Visit an Orthodox service	

21	Watch a birth	✳ _____
22	Conquer your fear	✳ _____
23	Grapple with Revelation	✳ _____
24	Be still	✳ _____
25	Grow something you eat	✳ _____
26	Blog	✳ _____
27	Write a letter to your future self	✳ _____
28	Have a conversation with the preacher	✳ _____
29	Write a hymn	✳ _____
30	Experience the taste of tea	✳ _____
31	Keep a Sabbath	✳ _____
32	Label your photographs	✳ _____
33	Plan a trip around the world	✳ _____
34	Create a memorial	✳ _____
35	Join a discussion group	✳ _____
36	Go Christmas caroling	✳ _____
37	Learn to sign	✳ _____
38	Make a family tree	✳ _____
39	Gaze at the night sky	✳ _____
40	Pray the rosary	✳ _____
41	Keep a spiritual journal	✳ _____
42	Learn about jazz	✳ _____
43	Plant a tree	✳ _____
44	Wash feet	✳ _____
45	Write a statement of faith	✳ _____
46	Help people register to vote	✳ _____
47	Take a new route to work	✳ _____
48	Walk the stations of the cross	✳ _____
49	Contribute to Wikipedia	✳ _____

50 Find out about Islam _____

51 Forgive a wrong _____

52 Learn yoga _____

53 Say grace _____

54 Investigate your Christian name _____

55 Learn the globe _____

56 Get acquainted with community help services _____

57 Listen to a choral masterpiece _____

58 Sell your possessions at a flea market _____

59 Have an alternative Christmas _____

60 Analyze yourself with Myers-Briggs _____

61 Give to the world's poorest people _____

62 Say the Jesus Prayer _____

63 Clear out the cupboards _____

64 Ride a roller coaster _____

65 Find your first home _____

66 Buy nothing for a day _____

67 Visit an ancient Christian site _____

68 Read religious poetry _____

69 Watch a different kind of movie _____

70 Invite your neighbors for a meal _____

71 Change the way you shop _____

72 Exercise _____

73 Observe Ash Wednesday _____

74 Go skinny-dipping _____

75 Visit an art gallery _____

76 Fast for a day _____

77 Send a virtual gift

78 Run a foot race

79 Investigate a saint

80 Help promote literacy

81 Pray in an airport chapel

82 Read the Bible from cover to cover

83 Make a sharing arrangement

84 Visit a nursing home

85 Collect for a charity

86 Pray in a cathedral

87 Make a confession

88 Learn the Seven Wonders of the Ancient World

89 Imagine yourself into a Bible story

90 Discover Celtic Christianity

91 Take part in a Passover meal

92 Write a prayer

93 Explore religions you know little about

94 Find out what you are worth

95 Watch an eclipse of the sun

96 Dance in the rain

97 Make your own Christmas cards

98 Hug someone

99 Plan your funeral

1 *Watch the sun rise*

How? Choose a vantage point where there is a good view of the horizon when you face east. Many places on the coast offer fine views eastward over the sea, but you could equally choose a hilltop looking over a city or fields. Since the middle of the eighteenth century, Christians have gathered on hilltops (originally cemeteries) in the early hours of Easter Sunday to praise the risen Jesus as the sun rises.

Use the Internet to find out when the sun will rise (visit www .weather.com, enter the location, and check the details which will give you the time of the sunrise for the next day). Be at the site an hour before that in order to appreciate the depth of darkness of the night and the changing colors and shades following the dawn. Wear warm clothes.

What Should I Expect? During a sunrise you may
find yourself reflecting on the goodness of God the creator, who has made the planet both complex and beautiful. The spectacular colors are due to an effect called Rayleigh scattering. Particles in our atmosphere cause the light of the sun, which is constantly white, to split into its component colors. The most common particles, oxygen and nitrogen, cause the light to be scattered at the frequency that we observe as being in the blue spectrum, so the sky appears blue when the sun is overhead. During sunrise, the distance the light travels to our eyes is greater, so the blue light is more scattered. As a result, more of the light from the red and orange spectrum reaches our eyes, sometimes with a dazzling impact.

Thank God that the display is constant and commonplace, but also magnificent and full of wonder—adjectives that could also describe God. The very same effect was observed by Jesus, by Abraham, and by prehistoric humans. God has been faithful and gracious to God's creation through all that time, as the earth has spun on its orbit of the sun. Our increased understanding of how it happens has only led to a greater awe of the God who imagined it into being.

DON'T

Don't be disappointed if an overcast sky means the colors are mainly gray. Clouds too are a wonder of God's creation.

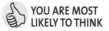 **YOU ARE MOST LIKELY TO THINK**

To have a God with the ability to create a world in which life is possible is wonderful; to have a God with the imagination to fill it with such beauty is stupendous.

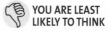 **YOU ARE LEAST LIKELY TO THINK**

The display in front of me is the result of the diffraction of light through the haphazard weather as the planet turns on its axis in this godless universe.

WHO SAYS?

Praised be you, my Lord, with all your creatures, especially Sir Brother Sun, who is the day and through whom you give us light. And he is beauiful and radiant with great splendors, and bears likeness of you, Most High One.

—Francis of Assisi, founder of the Franciscan order, 1182–1226

To Help You Reflect

Come, let us return to the LORD.
He has torn us to pieces but he will heal us;
he has injured us but he will bind up our wounds....
Let us press on to acknowledge him.
As surely as the sun rises, he will appear;
he will come to us like the winter rains, like the
spring rains that water the earth.

Hosea 6:1, 3

[Give the Lord's] people the knowledge of salvation
through the forgiveness of their sins,
because of the tender mercy of our God,
by which the rising sun will come to us from heaven
to shine on those living in darkness
and in the shadow of death,
to guide our feet into the path of peace.

Luke 1:77–79

The date I saw the sun rise:

Where, and who else was there?

The colors I saw:

What I will remember between here and heaven:

2 *Bake bread*

How? Gather the ingredients: sugar, dried yeast, flour, milk, salt, vegetable oil. You will need a dry cup measure, a liquid cup measure, a tablespoon, a sturdy wooden spoon, a large mixing bowl, and two loaf pans. First, put one cup of warm water plus one tablespoon of sugar in a mixing bowl. Add two tablespoons of yeast, and let it sit for about five minutes. Mix three cups of flour with a dash of salt and two tablespoons of sugar. Add this to the yeast mixture, along with one cup of milk and three to four tablespoons of oil (use melted and cooled margarine or shortening if you prefer). Stir the dough fifty times clockwise, then fifty times counterclockwise. Add another three to four cups of flour and mix until the dough forms a good ball. Turn the dough out of the bowl onto a floured surface and let it sit for ten minutes. Then knead the dough for five to ten minutes. Place in a greased bowl. Set the bowl of dough in a warm place and let it rise for about an hour, until it doubles in size. Punch down the dough. Let it rise again for thirty to forty-five minutes. Divide into two equal parts and shape into loaves. Place in greased loaf pans and bake at 425 degrees for twenty-five to thirty minutes. To check if the loaves are fully baked, remove them from the pans. The loaves should feel firm, and you should hear a hollow sound when you tap them on the bottom. Place the loaves on a wire rack to cool for fifteen to twenty minutes. If you don't do this, the bread will become doughy when you cut into it.

Now comes the best part: invite someone to share the bread with you. Sharing fresh-baked bread with others is one of life's truest pleasures!

What Should I Expect? People find baking bread a surprisingly spiritual experience. Shared with others, newly baked bread has echoes of Communion. It is not by accident that Jesus asked to be remembered by shared bread—an ancient, worldwide food formed out of the simplest ingredients. Like him, it is life-giving. In the Bible it is a symbol of humankind's most basic needs, both physical and spiritual. So there is something timeless and satisfying in creating and sharing it, whether you thump more anger or love into the kneading.

DON'T

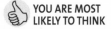 **YOU ARE MOST LIKELY TO THINK**

 **YOU ARE LEAST LIKELY TO THINK**

Don't feel you have had the same experience if you use a bread-making machine. You need to sink your hands in the dough.

Ah, that smell! Please pass the loaf.

This is the best thing since sliced bread.

WHO SAYS?

The time I spend baking bread has become a time for me to see the beauty and hope in chaos. When I bake, I am certain to make a mess, to have flour up to my elbows, and dough turning to paste on the hairs of my arms. Yet baking is also about precision—the grammes and ounces that keep me grounded. Baking a loaf of bread is esoteric and mundane. It is divine and it is earthy. It is eternal, and it will turn to dust.

> —*Alice Downs, priest and cook, writing in* Leaven for Our Lives

To Help You Reflect

He who supplies seed to the sower and bread for food will also supply and increase your store of seed and will enlarge the harvest of your righteousness.

2 Corinthians 9:10

[Jesus] told them still another parable: "The kingdom of heaven is like yeast that a woman took and mixed into a large amount of flour until it worked all through the dough."

Matthew 13:33

The date I baked bread:

The people I shared the bread with:

The comments they made:

What I will remember between here and heaven:

3 Read a Gospel in one sitting

How? Curl up in an armchair and open a Bible as if you were opening a novel. Choose Mark's Gospel because it is the shortest. Surround yourself with chocolate, drinks, or whatever would usually accompany an evening's entertainment. Try to pretend that you don't know how it ends.

What Should I Expect?

This is the story of the life of Jesus read in the way it was intended to be read. The chapters and verses that divide up the text were introduced in the thirteenth and sixteenth centuries respectively. The Gospel writers first presented their work as seamless and searing stories of three years in the life of someone whom they admired beyond measure. Two of them (Matthew and Luke) also provided a prologue by researching Jesus' birth.

For thirty years after Jesus' resurrection almost nothing was written down about his life, because most of the eyewitnesses were illiterate, and because they expected Jesus to return to earth in person any day. Stories were passed on by word of mouth. It was only as a generation of children grew up who had not met Jesus that the need for a written record became apparent. Many accounts were written, some of which can still be read even though they are not in the Bible. As you would expect of stories that were passed from person to person, some had wild exaggerations. There was a serious job of research and clarification to be done, drawing together the information and sorting fact from fantasy. By AD 150, four accounts had emerged as reliable.

Mark's Gospel is full of action, racing through Jesus' life. Matthew based his account on Mark's, expanding it to explain how Jesus fulfilled all that the Old Testament anticipated. Luke is more of a teacher, also enlarging Mark's account to stress the salvation that Jesus had brought. John, writing later, goes deeper in explaining how Jesus' life and teaching reveal God.

DON'T

Don't break your reading up into little sections, as daily Bible reading plans tend to. Instead, take in the entire, compelling sweep of his life in its excitement, tragedy and triumph.

YOU ARE MOST LIKELY TO THINK

Such a burning compassion. Such a loving mind. Such a Technicolor imagination. Such a strong will. Such a rebellious nature. Such a sacrificial life.

YOU ARE LEAST LIKELY TO THINK

Just as I remember from a child's first book of Bible stories—worthy, saintly, and bland.

To Help You Reflect

Many have undertaken to draw up an account of the things that have been fulfilled among us, just as they were handed down to us by those who from the first were eyewitnesses and servants of the word. Therefore, since I myself have carefully investigated everything from the beginning, it seemed good also to me to write an orderly account for you, most excellent Theophilus, so that you may know the certainty of the things you have been taught.
Luke 1:1–4

Jesus did many other miraculous signs in the presence of his disciples, which are not recorded in this book. But these are written that you may believe that Jesus is the Christ, the Son of God, and that by believing you may have life in his name.
John 20:30, 31

The date I read a complete Gospel:

Which one?

Something I noticed about Jesus that I had not recognized before:

What I will remember between here and heaven:

4 Give blood

How? Every two seconds, someone in the United States needs blood. By giving blood, you may help save a life.

The American Red Cross provides information about blood donation, as well as locations where you can give blood, including mobile blood banks. Check the Web site www.givelife.org, or call 1-800-GIVELIFE (1-800-448-3543). This site also has information about blood, blood types, and why giving blood is so important.

If you have questions about giving blood, please search out the answers, for you may indeed qualify to be a blood donor. With only 5 percent of the population giving blood on a regular basis, the need for more donors is huge.

What Should I Expect?

A nurse will ask you some questions and invite you to fill in a form. He or she will then take one drop of blood from the end of your finger, which will be tested to check that you are well enough to donate blood and to identify your blood type. You then lie on a couch, while the nurse slides a needle painlessly into a vein in your arm. For about ten minutes you chat while a pint of blood is taken. The needle is then removed, and you will be invited to sit and have refreshments so that you spend a few minutes at a slower pace instead of rushing away. You will get a card that thanks you and invites you to return four months later. Your body will replace the quantity of blood within a day and its richness within a week.

This is an immensely practical way of showing the love for our fellow human beings that Jesus selected as one of the two most important commandments. Bringing healing has always been a sign that the kingdom of God is present, so you can expect to feel that you have joined Jesus in the task of doing God's work in the world. Enjoy the fact that giving blood is an act of generosity, and that (unlike in some countries) there is no payment to change it into merely a commercial transaction.

The writers of the Old Testament believed that blood contained all the substances that made the difference between life and death. This led to them treating blood with great honor, particularly in the sacrifice of animals. Some religious groups interpret this as forbidding blood transfusions, but for most Christians, the opportunity to give life seems a precious gift.

DON'T Don't donate blood if you are under 17 or over 60, if you are pregnant or ill (the Web site is more specific). And don't put others at risk by donating blood if, during the past year, you have visited a country where malaria is common, or had a tattoo or body piercing.

 **YOU ARE MOST LIKELY TO THINK**

Is that all there is to it?

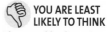 **YOU ARE LEAST LIKELY TO THINK**

I hope my blood goes to someone of whom I approve.

To Help You Reflect

David praised the LORD . . . "Who am I, and who are my people, that we should be able to give as generously as this? Everything comes from you, and we have given only what comes from your hand."

1 Chronicles 29:14

You will be made rich in every way so that you can be generous on every occasion, and through us your generosity will result in thanksgiving to God. This service that you perform is not only supplying the needs of God's people but is also overflowing in many expressions of thanks to God.

2 Corinthians 9:11–12

The date I donated my blood:

Where?

These were my thoughts as it happened:

What I will remember between here and heaven:

5 *Examine an icon*

How? There are three ways to examine icons—by participating in an act of worship at an Orthodox church, by visiting an art gallery, or by looking at pictures in a book or on the Internet.

In Orthodox practice, icons are provided to be worshiped (which is distinct from being adored, as only God can be). An icon is more than a religious painting. It is created as an act of prayer to precise specifications, using techniques and materials in a way that has not changed for centuries. Opening yourself to God in the presence of an icon is a way of encountering, in a sense, the actual presence of the subject that has been painted, so doing this in a church as part of an act of worship is by far the most valuable way.

Art galleries and museums may bring in a special collection of icons from other countries, and this is an ideal opportunity to examine an actual historical icon (for an example, check the Web site of The Getty, a museum in Los Angeles: www.getty.edu). Seeing an icon that has been in existence for centuries will be different from examining a copy of an icon, but if you are unable to see an actual display, that should not hold you back from using another form, such as a reproduction in a book or a replica. You can search the Web for sites that offer these for sale.

Frederica Mathewes-Green's book *The Open Door: Entering the Sanctuary of Icons and Prayer* (2003, Paraclete Press) offers a wonderful explanation of the history and spiritual enrichment provided by icons. The book includes paintings and drawings of icons, and a step-by-step guide to understanding twelve particular icons throughout the course of a year.

What Should I Expect? Stand in front of the icon, relax, and invite God to speak to you through it. Notice the way that inverse perspective is used so that objects that are close are painted smaller than those that are far away. The effect of this is to draw you into the picture, as if you are looking not only at the surface, but through it into the reality beyond. Look at the face portrayed, and ask yourself what mood it is inviting worshipers to assume. All the other elements of the painting (clothes, objects, colors, poses) have been put there deliberately. Why? Can the icon teach you about your place in the world? Can it point you to God, or challenge you to emulate the subject?

YOU ARE MOST LIKELY TO THINK

What I can see is beautiful, but there are things that God has put in this world that are real, but which I cannot see. In time, I want to appreciate that they are beautiful too.

YOU ARE LEAST LIKELY TO THINK

Mickey Mouse is an icon too. I wonder which will have a more lasting impact on me.

! DON'T   Don't rush.

WHO SAYS?

Icons are a true mirror of the divine. They are a window into heaven. What I love is the stillness of them; the fact that we venerate them as if they were real presences. They have a quality that does not demand anything of you. They are there, saying, "Take me if you want." They are a vessel through which the Holy Spirit might be able to talk.

John Tavener, composer

To Help You Reflect

The Lord has chosen Bezalel son of Uri, the son of Hur, of the tribe of Judah, and he has filled him with the Spirit of God, with skill, ability and knowledge in all kinds of crafts—to make artistic designs for work in gold, silver and bronze, to cut and set stones, to work in wood and to engage in all kinds of artistic craftsmanship . . . just as the Lord has commanded.

Exodus 35:30–36:1

This is what I seek:
that I may dwell in the house of the Lord
    all the days of my life,
to gaze upon the beauty of the Lord
and to seek him in his temple.

Psalm 27:4

The date I spent time in front of an icon:

What was the subject portrayed?

Details and truths of which I became aware:

What I will remember between here and heaven:

---

6 *Give your testimony*

How? Your testimony is the true story of the difference that God has made to your life. Telling other people this story can bring great encouragement to fellow Christians, and can show people who do not have an active faith that following Jesus is normal, rewarding, and worth considering for themselves. Ask a church leader whether a suitable occasion might arise to tell publicly the story of how you have come to put your faith in God. He or she may recommend giving your testimony to a small group connected with the church, or may suggest that it would be appropriate to tell your story during a church service.

To prepare your testimony, think about and write down the main reason that you are a follower of Jesus. Is there an anecdote attached, or was it a growing realization? Who or what helped you understand? What differences are you aware of in your lifestyle and priorities before and after your faith became real? Give as much interesting detail as you can, but don't exaggerate or make yourself seem like a hero.

You don't have to tell your entire life story or say everything that is significant to you as a Christian. You could give a testimony about just one thing that has happened to you (for example, about how the birth of a grandson made you think about what kind of world you want him to grow up in). Save the rest of your life story as a treat for another occasion. There is no rule that dictates what your testimony must be like, but it should definitely encourage your listeners by showing that trust in Jesus has had a positive impact on your life.

What Should I Expect? People are fascinated by stories like these because a testimony is a real account of struggle and hope. It doesn't explain what happens in theory; it shows what takes place in reality.

To tell the story of your life "warts and all" makes you very vulnerable. However, it is that vulnerability that people find so compelling. It helps them realize that the difficulties they experience in believing in God are not unique to them. It gives them confidence to trust. So expect to be warmly thanked for sharing your story and to feel that you have done more to introduce people to Jesus than a library full of books.

DON'T Don't use Christian jargon like "born again" or "converted," which has no meaning to people who are not used to going to church. Find ways of explaining what those things mean in practice.

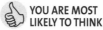

YOU ARE MOST LIKELY TO THINK

They must all think what a great God I follow.

YOU ARE LEAST LIKELY TO THINK

They must all think what a great person I am.

To Help You Reflect

Always be prepared to give an answer to everyone who asks you to give the reason for the hope that you have. But do this with gentleness and respect, keeping a clear conscience, so that those who speak maliciously against your good behavior in Christ may be ashamed of their slander.

1 Peter 3:15–16

We are therefore Christ's ambassadors, as though God were making his appeal through us. We implore you on Christ's behalf: Be reconciled to God.

2 Corinthians 5:20

The date I gave my testimony:

What was the setting?

The most important thing I said:

What I will remember between here and heaven:

7 Learn a musical instrument

How? Choose the instrument that you would like to learn for social reasons (because playing drums in a band or cello in an orchestra is creatively rewarding), for practical reasons (because a guitar fits better in the elevator to a tenth-floor apartment than a piano), or simply because the instrument intrigues you (a harp sounds gorgeous anywhere).

If you have left school, the most reliable way to find a teacher is by word of mouth. Other ways of making contact are through the lists that most music shops keep, or via www.privatelessons.com. There is no substitute for putting in regular practice, and most adults take up music because they want to play, not because they need another qualification.

What Should I Expect?

All civilizations of history have used music to lead them beyond the everyday toward the divine. Christianity, and before that Judaism, have particularly embraced music as a means of worshiping God and seen musical talent as a gift that he alone can give. This is true whenever music is made, not just when it is used in the context of organized worship.

Of course, instruments can be used for music in a way that diverts people's attention from God (which is why the Puritans decided in the seventeenth century to ban them and praise God with voices alone). However, by being a person who creates, rather than just consumes, music, you become part of an activity that touches people in a way that neither thoughts nor words alone could. You are at the heart of something that communicates insights beyond materialism and puts people in touch with deep spiritual values. More than a personal achievement, more than a lasting joy, more than shared pleasure, you are showing why you are in the image of God. You are becoming creative, like your Creator.

DON'T

Don't attempt to use "teach yourself" books and manage without a teacher unless you are naturally gifted and determined. (Drums and guitars are possible exceptions.)

 **YOU ARE MOST LIKELY TO THINK**

Mozart, Mendelssohn, Mahler, me—we have one thing in common.

YOU ARE LEAST LIKELY TO THINK

Mozart, Mendelssohn, Mahler, me—we have many things in common.

To Help You Reflect

It is good to praise the LORD
and make music to your name, O Most High,
to proclaim your love in the morning
and your faithfulness at night,
to the music of the ten-stringed lyre
and the melody of the harp.
For you make me glad by your deeds, O LORD;
I sing for joy at the works of your hands.

Psalm 92:1–4

[David selected performers who] were under the supervision of their fathers for the music of the temple of the LORD, with cymbals, lyres and harps, for the ministry at the house of God ... Along with their relatives—all of them trained and skilled in music for the LORD—they numbered 288. Young and old alike ...

1 Chronicles 25:6–8

The date I took up a musical instrument:

Which instrument and why?

A new composer I have come to admire:

What I will remember between here and heaven:

8 *Learn about Judaism*

How? Day-to-day life for the Jewish people is rooted in the Torah (the first five books of the Bible) and shaped by the laws and traditions of the faith community.

Judaism 101 has a fine Web site dedicated to helping non-Jews understand the beliefs, practices, and history of the Jews. At its online encyclopedia, you can choose to read basic, intermediate, or advanced information. Visit www.jewfaq.org and click "Table of contents."

Helpful books include *Judaism, a Very Short Introduction* (Norman Solomon, Oxford Paperbacks) and *Jewish Spirituality: A Brief Introduction for Christians* (Lawrence Kushner, Jewish Lights Publishing).

The National Museum of American Jewish History (www.nmajh.org) has links to Jewish museums and museum resources worldwide.

Encourage your pastor to set up a meeting between congregations with a local Jewish leader. A healthy exchange of ideas and an interfaith dialogue on a particular topic of mutual interest would be welcomed by many people. Such a gathering could also look for ways to work together in community service or relief efforts.

To find out more about Judaism and to locate a synagogue in your area, go to www.beliefnet.com. Some synagogues may welcome visitors, but for reasons of security and good etiquette, you should phone ahead and set up an appropriate time to visit. Again, perhaps this can be something you do as a group with your church family, under the guidance of your pastor.

What Should I Expect? Expect to discover a

community in which some practice their religion faithfully while others are secular, but strongly regard themselves as part of a people with a unique identity. Core beliefs are that there is one, all-powerful God who created the universe and has a unique relationship with the Jewish people. Devout Jews long for the coming of the Messiah, God's anointed one, who will inaugurate an era of peace. (Christians believe Jesus to have fulfilled this.)

We should celebrate and honor the Jewish heritage in its own right, not just as part of our Christian history.

DON'T Don't make the mistake of assuming that the word "Israel" in the Bible refers to the present-day secular state of "Israel." To do so without taking into account what God has done over two thousand subsequent years has led to some Christians lending their support to actions that have caused suffering in the Middle East.

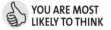 **YOU ARE MOST LIKELY TO THINK**

These are the deep and precious roots of my Christian faith.

 **YOU ARE LEAST LIKELY TO THINK**

Jesus was a Christian.

WHO SAYS?

If something is hateful to you, do not do it to your neighbor. This is the whole of the Jewish law. The rest is merely commentary. Go and study it!

Hillel the Elder, Jewish theologian about 70 BC–AD 10

To Help You Reflect

I will tell of the kindnesses of the LORD,
the deeds for which he is to be praised,
according to all the LORD has done for us—
yes, the many good things he has done
  for the house of Israel,
according to his compassion and many
  kindnesses.
He said, "Surely they are my people,
sons who will not be false to me";
and so he became their Savior.

Isaiah 63:7–8

The date I learned about Judaism:

How?

Something I learned that changed me:

What I will remember between here and heaven:

9 *Help fight poverty through microfinance*

How? Many people feel strongly about using their financial resources to make the world a better place for others. One way to do this is through microfinance.

Before investing in any altruistic endeavor, it is important to understand how an agency or system works. If you are not familiar with the idea of microfinance, take some time to do research through Web sites, financial institutions, and conversations with people you trust.

Microfinancing reaches out to those who cannot obtain loans, insurance, assets, and other monetary securities. Through microfinance, people living in poverty or without resources are given hope for independent living that would otherwise be outside their reach. Microfinancing provides opportunities for individuals, families, and communities that cannot afford the basics.

Global Partnerships (www.globalpartnerships.org) is an officially recognized 501(c)(3) nonprofit organization and a leader in providing microfinance opportunities for the people of Latin America. Its Web site provides information about the concept and the process of investing in microfinance.

The income that is generated through micro-loans provides for better food, health care, and education, enhancing the quality of life for a multitude of people and providing hope for the present as well as for the future of God's children everywhere.

What Should I Expect?

As you investigate microfinance, your eyes will be opened to opportunities for outreach you may never have imagined. You will discover that even a very small donation can have an amazing impact in the lives of people throughout the world. You don't have to have a multitude of financial resources to make a difference in someone else's life.

DON'T

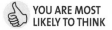 **YOU ARE MOST LIKELY TO THINK**

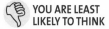 **YOU ARE LEAST LIKELY TO THINK**

Don't stop at learning microfinance yourself. Let others know how they can invest, too.

I am rich in so many ways.

Everybody else has more than I do; let them be the ones who give.

WHO SAYS?

Every charitable act is a stepping stone towards heaven.
—*Henry Ward Beecher, American clergyman and reformer*

To Help You Reflect

If you do good to those who are good to you, what credit is that to you? Even "sinners" do that. And if you lend to those from whom you expect repayment, what credit is that to you? Even "sinners" lend to "sinners," expecting to be repaid in full. But love your enemies, do good to them, and lend to them without expecting to get anything back.... Be merciful, just as your Father is merciful. Do not judge, and you will not be judged. Do not condemn, and you will not be condemned. Forgive, and you will be forgiven. Give, and it will be given to you. A good measure, pressed down, shaken together and running over, will be poured into your lap. For with the measure you use, it will be measured to you.

Luke 6:33–38

The date I learned about microfinance:

What and where I decided to invest:

How I felt after choosing to participate:

What I will remember between here and heaven:

10 *Go on a protest rally*

How? Causes that attract Christians to campaign in large numbers are those that uphold the values of the kingdom of God. When they are moved to take to the streets, it is on behalf of poor people who are denied justice, oppressed people who need release, or war-scarred people who seek peace. Rallies that are worth supporting are well organized and have a specific message to communicate to those with the power to bring change.

Visit the Web site of the organization that is planning the rally. Make sure you know and understand its objective. (If it is unclear, the event is probably not worth supporting.) Find out the time and place, and make sure that there is a map that shows the route of any march that is planned and the location of performances and speeches. Satisfy yourself that care has been taken over the safety of the event (for instance, the provision of toilets, facilities for disabled people, first aid, and attendants). Well in advance, investigate travel and accommodation, so that there is no danger of you getting stranded. Take appropriate clothes and shoes for the weather that is expected, and carry food and water.

Take something with you that shows what cause you are supporting (a placard or T-shirt, for instance), and join in enthusiastically and noisily.

What Should I Expect?

The irony of protest rallies that support the values of the kingdom of God is that although the cause is concerned with tragedy, the event is usually exhilarating. It is uplifting to join large numbers of Christians who are committed to taking action on behalf of suffering people. And discovering a common cause with people of other faiths or no faith expands your understanding of the vast scale on which God is working in his kingdom.

Expect speeches that clarify the importance of opposing evil, and joyful music that allows your heart to be as excited about addressing injustice as your head. Seek out acts of worship (always present, but sometimes hard to find) that allow you to pray quietly and seriously among the clamor. Many rallies include a march (more often a stroll) that makes your act of Christian witness public. Official marches have always arranged the cooperation of the police in advance and are safe and peaceful.

DON'T

Don't defy a policeman, damage anyone's property, behave in a way that will bring the good cause you are supporting into disrepute, or do anything else likely to lead to your arrest.

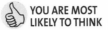 **YOU ARE MOST LIKELY TO THINK**

In the New Testament, James tells us that faith without actions is dead. Today my faith really is alive and making a difference to the world.

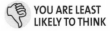 **YOU ARE LEAST LIKELY TO THINK**

I really should have stayed home and kept up to date with the soaps.

To Help You Reflect

[Jeremiah protested:] "Whenever I speak, I cry out proclaiming violence and destruction. So the word of the LORD has brought me insult and reproach all day long. But if I say, 'I will not mention him or speak any more in his name,' his word is in my heart like a fire, a fire shut up in my bones. I am weary of holding it in; indeed, I cannot."

Jeremiah 20:8–9

[Approaching Jerusalem], the whole crowd of disciples began joyfully to praise God in loud voices. . . . Some of the Pharisees in the crowd said to Jesus, "Teacher, rebuke your disciples!" "I tell you," he replied, "if they keep quiet, the stones will cry out." As he approached Jerusalem and saw the city, he wept over it.

Luke 19:37–41

The date and place I attended a protest rally:

The just cause about which I was demonstrating:

What changed (in the world or in me) as a result of the demonstration?

What I will remember between here and heaven:

11 *Revisit your childhood self*

How? Find a comfortable place and prepare for a meditation. Unlike a daydream, you will guide what you think about, not just let random thoughts occur.

Imagine yourself in a beautiful, spacious place—one that you have actually visited and in which you have been happy. Walk through it alone. Enjoy the view. Think about the care with which God has created this place and the way he fills every aspect of it. As you stroll, become aware of another figure in the far distance. The figure is too far away to identify, but it is a human. As it approaches, become conscious that the person is the same gender as you, although much younger. It is a young child. Walk on, until you are close enough to identify features. It is you.

Draw near and greet your childhood self. Remind yourself what life was like at that age. Then, taking stock of all that has happened to you subsequently, tell your childhood self the things you would like him or her to know about what lies ahead and how to be prepared for them. Take time over this. In your imagination, give an expression of affection to the child in the way you would most like to have been loved when you were that age. Turn around, walk away, and bring yourself back to the realities of the room you are in.

What Should I Expect?

You are the same person that you were as a child, and things that happened then have shaped the way you are today. The child that you once were can be spiritual, playful, and spontaneous, but he or she can also be fearful and critical. Knowing that can help you understand why you are attracted to certain people or react in particular ways. It can reveal the logic of what makes you scared, angry, or lonely. When you know that, you can benefit from it or control it so that it does not trap you.

Throughout this meditation, keep the presence of God closely in your thoughts. You are not attempting to heal yourself; you are opening an opportunity for God (and God alone) to heal you. The least you can expect is some interesting memories; the most you can expect is for God to develop a more wise, liberated, and loving you.

DON'T

Don't reopen distressing memories unless you are in a position to deal with the feelings. If you are seeking to heal deep wounds you need the guidance of someone experienced. To find help, contact the American Association of Christian Counselors at www.aacc.net.

 **YOU ARE MOST LIKELY TO THINK**

I need not be imprisoned. In God there is healing.

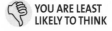 **YOU ARE LEAST LIKELY TO THINK**

What a horrible little brat!

To Help You Reflect

When I was a child, I talked like a child, I thought like a child, I reasoned like a child. When I became a man, I put childish ways behind me. Now we see but a poor reflection as in a mirror; then we shall see face to face. Now I know in part; then I shall know fully, even as I am fully known. And now these three remain: faith, hope and love. But the greatest of these is love.

1 Corinthians 13:11–13

When I was a boy in my father's house, still tender, and an only child of my mother, he taught me and said, "Lay hold of my words with all your heart; keep my commands and you will live. . . . Do not forsake wisdom, and she will protect you; love her, and she will watch over you."

Proverbs 4:3–6

The date I revisited my childhood self:

What advice would the mature me give to the child I was?

What changes might I make?

What I will remember between here and heaven:

12 Take part in a Tenebrae service

How? Tenebrae means shadows. It is an evening service that takes place on one of the days immediately before Easter, using darkness as a way of focusing your mind on the horror of Jesus' crucifixion. If the church you attend does not offer a Tenebrae service, you can find one by checking your local newspaper for churches that offer this deeply meaningful worship.

What Should I Expect?

This is an unremittingly solemn service that allows you to enter into the emotions surrounding the crucifixion of Jesus. There is no happy ending. It leaves you in a darkness and despair that will not be relieved until Easter morning dawns.

The service begins with a somber mood, achieved through the choice of music, Scripture readings, and the appearance of the sanctuary. In some cases, the sanctuary is stripped of color and décor. Candles are lit, and then extinguished after each of the Scripture readings. The readings all focus on the trial, crucifixion, and death of Jesus.

After the final candle is extinguished, there may be a time of silence or special music. The congregation leaves the service in darkness and silence.

You will find this one of the most moving services of the year. Because it is unremittingly bleak, without a hint of resurrection, it will remind you that the first followers of Jesus witnessed his death without the advantage we have of knowing that new life was to follow. The style of the service acknowledges that suffering is a reality of existence for every human because it is a reality for God. Only by dwelling on the awfulness of Jesus' anguish is it possible fully to experience the joy of Easter morning.

DON'T

Don't talk to anyone as you leave the service. Go to bed with the darkness and wretchedness vivid in your mind.

 **YOU ARE MOST LIKELY TO THINK**

I have had a glimpse at the utter desolation of a world in which God has died.

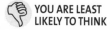 **YOU ARE LEAST LIKELY TO THINK**

All Christian worship is joyous and uplifting.

WHO SAYS?

Good Captain, maker of
    the light,
Who dost divide the day
    and night,
The sun is drowned
    beneath the sea,
Chaos is on us horribly:
O Christ, give back to
    faithful souls the light.
Prudentius, Spanish poet,
in a prayer for Easter Eve,
348–410

To Help You Reflect

Jesus said to the chief priests, the officers of the temple guard, and the elders, who had come for him . . . "Every day I was with you in the temple courts, and you did not lay a hand on me. But this is your hour—when darkness reigns." Then seizing him, they led him away and took him into the house of the high priest.   Luke 22:52–54

Those crucified with [Jesus] also heaped insults on him. At the sixth hour darkness came over the whole land until the ninth hour. And at the ninth hour Jesus cried out in a loud voice, "Eloi, Eloi, lama sabachthani?"—which means, "My God, my God, why have you forsaken me?" . . . With a loud cry, Jesus breathed his last.
                    Mark 15:32–34, 37

The date I attended a Tenebrae service:

Where?

What happened that was unlike a usual service?

What I will remember between here and heaven:

13 *Bury a time capsule*

How? The first modern attempt to preserve objects for a future generation was in 1939 at the New York World's Fair. Seeds, a doll, newsreel, a microscope, and statistical information are buried under Flushing Meadow awaiting 6939.

You could create a small time capsule with children for them to open in their old age. Choose objects that are of personal interest, such as photographs, toys, and letters. Alternatively, involve a community group in creating a capsule for a future century, which contains objects that are representative of today's culture. Exclude objects containing rubber, wool, PVC, or anything edible unless you package them in such a way as to stop them giving off gas and causing other items to perish. If you choose something operated by electricity, leave details of the technology required, because the hardware will become a museum piece. Include a list of the contents, their color and significance, and keep another copy in a safe place.

Hold a "sealing ceremony" and place the capsule in a dark, dry place. Appoint an archivist whose responsibility is passing on the location to the next generation. Register what you have done with the International Time Capsule Society (find "International Time Capsule Society" at www.oglethorpe.edu).

What Should I Expect? A time capsule focuses
your mind on what is important about today's culture by prompting you to imagine life in the future. Select items that will demonstrate to a future age what is good and beautiful about this decade, as well as cheap objects that give a sense of everyday life. Identify things in your home that would have astonished nineteenth-century ancestors, and take ideas from them. As you do so, register the many ways in which the world has gotten better over the last century and thank God for them. Cynicism about a world going to the dogs will become impossible. And you will find energy for passing on the good news of Jesus to the next generation, knowing that his presence will enrich the lives of your descendants in as real a way as he has yours.

DON'T

Don't bury it in the ground, where damp will ruin the contents and you are likely to forget it.

 **YOU ARE MOST LIKELY TO THINK**

I hope that the people who open this live in a good and safe world, and have put their faith in Jesus Christ.

 **YOU ARE LEAST LIKELY TO THINK**

Nothing changes.

WHO SAYS?

We are blessing everything to be put into the time capsule on 29 December 2003. We have built the Kingdom of God on the foundation laid by those who preceded us. You in your day are a continuation of the journey through time of the people of God in this part of the world, all living, working and praising God for his glory. We pray that we will one day meet in the eternal life won for us by our Lord Jesus Christ.

John Steinbock, Bishop of Fresno, California, in a letter to his successor who in 2103 will open the capsule buried on the occasion of the centenary of St. John's Cathedral

To Help You Reflect

Let this be written for a future generation,
that a people not yet created may praise the LORD....
"In the beginning you laid the foundations of the earth,
and the heavens are the work of your hands.
They will perish, but you remain;
they will all wear out like a garment.
Like clothing you will change them and they will be discarded.
But you remain the same, and your years will never end."
Psalm 102:18, 25–27

The date I buried a time capsule:

Its location and the date I anticipate it will be opened:

The objects I have put in it:

What I will remember between here and heaven:

14 *Break a bad habit*

How? Begin by keeping track of the behavior that has become habitual. Keep a diary so that you know what prompts it. For instance, what triggers you biting your nails or chewing your cheek? Is there a pattern to the occasions when you feel an urge to smoke a cigarette or access an Internet site that is doing you no good? As your awareness of this increases, analyze what your feelings are as you succumb to the habit. What in your life is the habit addressing? Is it perhaps boredom, anger, stress, loneliness, anxiety?

Think of something you could do that is a more positive way of dealing with those feelings than the way that has become your automatic response. For example, massaging your palm instead of biting your nails, eating a piece of fruit instead of smoking (one that requires two hands to peel or prepare it), visiting an online chess game instead of an online chatroom. Try to catch yourself indulging in the behavior you want to change, and immediately substitute the alternative. Practice your new behavior in the hope that it will become habitual too. Tell everyone you know what you are doing and what they can do to help you.

If the bad habit indicates a more serious problem—an obsessive-compulsive disorder, for instance, or a response to a childhood trauma—seek counseling to deal with the difficulty.

What Should I Expect? There are some cravings that God has built into the way he created us, for example, needing water, sleep, or a loving touch. These are almost invariably life-enhancing. But there are other cravings that are artificial or adopted, and these can become destructive habits—eating until you are uncomfortably full, smoking, or hurting yourself (even in minor ways like pulling hairs out). You do not have to do these things. But the only way to stop yourself is to be convinced that you don't want to do them (which is different from knowing that you ought not to do them).

Friends, prayer, and rewarding yourself for small successes will all help. However, a change of attitude is the most important element of a change of behavior. See it as part of the process of becoming more fully human, and feeling increasingly like the delightful person God has always seen when God looks at you.

DON'T

Don't beat yourself up if you lapse—that's just another bad habit. Instead, have a quiet conversation with yourself and start the process again.

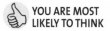 **YOU ARE MOST LIKELY TO THINK**

I am a strong person, and I shall now use that strength in a good way.

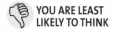 **YOU ARE LEAST LIKELY TO THINK**

That was easy!

To Help You Reflect

I have the desire to do what is good, but I cannot carry it out. For what I do is not the good I want to do; no, the evil I do not want to do—this I keep on doing.... What a wretched man I am! Who will rescue me from this body of death? Thanks be to God—through Jesus Christ our Lord!

Romans 7:18–19, 24–25

You ... were called to be free. But do not use your freedom to indulge the sinful nature; rather, serve one another in love.

Galatians 5:13

The date I broke a bad habit:

The behavior I changed:

The process I went through to break this behavior:

What I will remember between here and heaven:

15 *Learn about New Testament Greek*

How? For those who study theology at a university or in preparation for ordination, training to read the New Testament in its original language will almost certainly form part of the curriculum. If you are interested in learning New Testament Greek for your own interest, a local Bible college or theological seminary may offer courses.

An interlinear Greek-English Bible offers a way to learn some of the nuances of the language without taking a full course. The English translation is included underneath or alongside the Greek version, and often a full, literal translation of the Greek is also on the page. By using this type of Bible, you can appreciate more fully the effort and difficulty of translating accurately from one language into another.

A taste of learning the language can be found at www.ntgreek .net, where a great deal of self-discipline could allow you to cover the equivalent of the first year of a Bible college course at no expense.

If you get on a roll with learning Greek, try Old Testament Hebrew next!

What Should I Expect? The New Testament was
written in Greek, and every translation into another language adds and loses something. For example, Jesus' claim to be "the bread of life" was full of meaning for his original followers. But bread is not the staple food in every country of the world. Japanese Christians know bread as the food that only foreigners eat. So in Japan, interpreters of the Bible have a choice between translating Jesus' words as, "I am the bread of life," which is accurate but misleading, or, "I am the rice of life," which conveys exactly what Jesus meant, but not what he said.

This is an extreme example of ten thousand choices that translators make in order to bring us the Bible in a form we can comprehend. Some are minor (should prices be given in ancient denarii or modern dollars?) and others major (did Jesus offer to save lives or to save souls, because the word he used can mean either?). Understanding the language is the way through which you can get closest to knowing the original intention of the writers of the Gospels and letters.

DON'T

Don't accidentally sign up for a course in classical Greek, which is a different language.

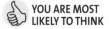 **YOU ARE MOST LIKELY TO THINK**

The language of the Gospels is more rich with meaning than I ever realized.

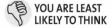 **YOU ARE LEAST LIKELY TO THINK**

Verily I say unto thee, only that which the King James Version saith is the Word of God.

WHO SAYS?

One of the many divine qualities of the Bible is this—that it does not yield its secrets to the irreverent and the censorious.

James Packer, theologian

To Help You Reflect

Our dear brother Paul [writes] with the wisdom that God gave him. He writes the same way in all his letters. . . . His letters contain some things that are hard to understand, which ignorant and unstable people distort, as they do the other Scriptures, to their own destruction. Therefore, dear friends, since you already know this, be on your guard.

2 Peter 3:15–17

[Paul wrote:] We do not write you anything you cannot read or understand. And I hope that, as you have understood us in part, you will come to understand fully that you can boast of us just as we will boast of you in the day of the LORD Jesus.

2 Corinthians 1:13–14

The date I started to learn New Testament Greek:

The course I am following:

The first words I learned, and their meanings:

What I will remember between here and heaven:

x
x
x

16 Milk a cow

How? First, the easy part: explaining how to milk a cow by hand. Put a stool next to the cow's udder and sit with your head resting on its flank. Clean the udder. Place a metal bucket under the teats. Take one teat in the palm of your hand. Squeeze it at the top with your thumb and forefinger, then progressively close the rest of your fingers around the teat, forcing the milk out in a stream. Release your grip and repeat it. When you are confident, use the other hand too, and develop a rhythm until the udder softens and the flow of milk declines.

Cows produce about 8 gallons of milk every day—enough to fill 100 glasses or 128 cups. They like routine, so it takes time for them to get used to a new person touching them. It may be better for an experienced person to start, before you take over. Try not to pull the teat or do anything else that will hurt the cow—it won't forget!

Next, the difficult part: finding a place where it is possible to learn the skill. Dairy farms are mechanized, and have large numbers of cattle. Milking a cow by hand will involve making a good relationship with a farmer who does not produce milk as a commercial venture, but has a small number of cows. It is sometimes possible to milk a cow on a farm that opens as a tourist attraction.

What Should I Expect?

Milk comes to us homogenized and pasteurized in a carton designed to pour easily. There is almost no tactile relationship with the natural world in the way we feed ourselves, so anything you can do to be more aware of the way you are connected to other living creatures is likely to enhance your appreciation of life.

The milk in the bucket under a cow has hair and hay (and worse) floating in it, which needs to be strained. It is a reminder that the world God has placed us in, although spectacular in its provision of good food, is full of mess and muddle. Giving humans the responsibility to farm and care for it is God's way of crafting an orderly environment in which every part of the creation is dependent on every other part in a delicate ecological balance. Divorcing yourself from that process makes it easier to damage the balance, and we do that at our peril.

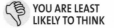

YOU ARE MOST LIKELY TO THINK

Now that the food I eat, packaged and processed, looks so little like the living organism from which it came, I must force myself to remember how dependent I am on those who farm God's land.

YOU ARE LEAST LIKELY TO THINK

Isn't farming romantic!

! DON'T

Don't forget that even nice cows kick!

WHO SAYS?

The cow is of the bovine ilk;
One end is moo, the other, milk.
Ogden Nash, poet, 1902–1971

To Help You Reflect

[The LORD will] send you rain for the seed you sow in the ground, and the food that comes from the land will be rich and plentiful. In that day your cattle will graze in broad meadows.

Isaiah 30:23

Godliness with contentment is great gain. For we brought nothing into the world, and we can take nothing out of it. But if we have food and clothing, we will be content with that.

1 Timothy 6:6–8

The date I milked a cow:

Where and what breed?

How much milk was produced?

What I will remember between here and heaven:

17 *Light a candle*

How? Put the candle in front of you in a safe setting. Light it. Begin by watching the flame and taking in its motion. Remind yourself that God the Holy Spirit is symbolized by flame, and be conscious that the Spirit is present with you. After a while begin to tell God of your fears, hopes, and joys. As the flame moves, be aware that God is alive and allow that truth to have an impact on the concerns that are in your mind.

What Should I Expect? Increasingly, lighted

candles are used to bring people together in moments of shared spirituality. They can be used to emphasize aspirations such as the release of hostages, justice for those who suffer, or public sorrow after a tragedy. It may be that you light a candle under those circumstances.

But equally, you may do this as a private act of devotion, since lighting a candle and then extinguishing it can mark the beginning and end of a personal prayer to God. It helps concentration to know that a specific period of time, while the flame burns, is marked out as special.

Lighting candles or lamps is a very ancient religious tradition. The Jews in the tabernacle, and then the Temple, made use of lamps, so it was not surprising that Christians in the years immediately after Jesus did the same, carrying lights into their evening service. The leaders of the church wrote about their importance not just to illuminate the room, but also to acknowledge their need for God to guide them, like a torch on a dark night, and to give them joy.

In Christian worship, candles have been used to recognize that Jesus called himself "the Light of the World." Candles have often been lit at moments when Jesus is recognized uniquely as the Lord, such as baptisms or Easter Sunday. Candles are also used by Christians to draw special attention to moments that require concentrated attention or honor, so many churches light candles at the start of an act of worship or make them prominent when the New Testament is read. Some also put them in places where their light reminds everyone of the importance of particular people and activities, such as in front of images of Jesus or saints, or the bread and wine of Communion.

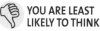

YOU ARE MOST LIKELY TO THINK

The entry of light will always change a dark place. But it is impossible for darkness ever to enter a place and extinguish the light. Knowing this makes it easier to believe that goodness will never be overcome by evil. Hope is imperishable.

YOU ARE LEAST LIKELY TO THINK

This place could do with some more noise and bustle.

DON'T

Don't leave a candle burning unattended.

To Help You Reflect

You, O LORD, keep my lamp burning;
my God turns my darkness into light.
With your help I can advance against a troop;
with my God I can scale a wall.
As for God, his way is perfect;
the word of the LORD is flawless.
He is a shield for all who take refuge in him.

Psalm 18:28–30

The light shines on in the dark, and the darkness has never mastered it.

John 1:5 NEB

The date I lit a candle as an act of devotion to God:

The color and shape of the candle:

The people and places in my mind as I reflected:

What I will remember between here and heaven:

18 *Go on a retreat*

How? A retreat is a planned time of spiritual refreshment in a beautiful setting. Because retreats are unhurried, they offer you a chance to reflect on the people and events that are significant in your life, to put them in the context of your experience of God, and to look ahead to the future. Usually a retreat involves sustained times of silence, which is the way many people are able to see past the surface of events and seek their meaning.

However, most retreats offer activity as well, in order to stimulate thoughts to dwell on in the silence. There may be a daily talk, or one-to-one meetings with someone who can guide you through the retreat and suggest what you might read or think about. On themed retreats you can be part of a group involved in a creative activity—for instance, painting, walking, or dance— bringing that experience into your prayer.

At www.retreats.org, you can find advertisements for Web sites that offer information on many different retreat opportunities. You might also search the Web for specific retreats, such as "writing retreats," to broaden your search for the retreat that is just the right fit for you.

What Should I Expect? Most lives are filled with
noise. Most waking hours are spent surrounded by people. Most days are dictated by the clock. A retreat allows you to see what happens if all three constraints are taken away. Many people find that they experience the presence of God in a revitalizing way.

This is not escapism, which would simply lead to you returning unchanged to the usual pressures. You bring the pressures and problems with you, but often discover that in a new and inspiring setting, previously unexplored ways of thinking about them open up. The circumstances that transform them can be as simple as a good night's sleep. But you will also be able to talk to someone wise, to pray in a different setting, and to know that no one requires you to meet a target or achieve a result. In circumstances in which you need to make a decision, or find courage and direction, a retreat is the setting in which God can allow those things to take place gently.

DON'T

Don't go with the expectation that others there will chat to you. If what you really seek is company, choose a group holiday rather than a retreat.

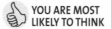 **YOU ARE MOST LIKELY TO THINK**

I am going to carry this refreshment with me back into my daily life, and God will give me the energy to do what is right and good.

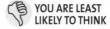 **YOU ARE LEAST LIKELY TO THINK**

I'm only fulfilled when I'm busy.

To Help You Reflect

Because so many people were coming and going that they did not even have a chance to eat, [Jesus] said to [his disciples], "Come with me by yourselves to a quiet place and get some rest." So they went away by themselves in a boat to a solitary place.

Mark 6:31–32

"Oh, that I had the wings of a dove!
I would fly away and be at rest—
I would flee far away and stay in the desert;
I would hurry to my place of shelter,
far from the tempest and storm. . . .
But I call to God, and the LORD saves me.
Evening, morning and noon I cry out in distress,
and he hears my voice.

Psalm 55:6–8, 16–17

The date I went on retreat:

Where?

My most significant thoughts:

What I will remember between here and heaven:

19 *Make a will*

How? Making a will usually involves an attorney. If your intentions for what should happen to your possessions after you die are simple (for instance, if you do not own property or intend to leave everything to one family member) you may be able to use a form on the Internet, and draw up the will yourself.

It is preferable to visit an attorney having thought in advance about what you want to happen to the things you own. Computer software for writing your will is available. Using it can help with the process, even if you end up going to an attorney to draw up the final papers.

If you die without making a will, there are legal rules that determine what happens, but it is quite possible that it will not be what you hoped or assumed would take place.

What Should I Expect? Make a list of your property,
savings, and objects that are important because they are valuable or loved. Decide to whom you would like to give all these things (they can be divided however you choose), and whether you would like to donate some to a charity. If you are a parent to children under 18, think about who will look after them. Decide on two people on whom you can rely to make sure these instructions are carried out (executors). Then ask two others to come and witness you signing the document (one can be the attorney, but neither should be people who will gain from your will).

The experience of making a will is both selfish and selfless—selfish because you can decide precisely what you want and no one (except in rare circumstances) can argue; selfless because it saves the people you love trauma and uncertainty at a time when they will be grieving that you are not present.

Although it deals with your death, you will not find yourself thinking morbidly. Instead you will be focusing on the people and things that bring you most happiness in life. It is a pleasure for most people to do this, knowing that its impact will be gratitude and joy. Treat it as an act of thanksgiving to God for all you enjoy about being alive.

Consider leaving a portion of your assets to a church or charity. This will create a lasting legacy and make a statement about what has been important to you.

 **YOU ARE MOST LIKELY TO THINK**

As a result of what I have just done, the sadness that is felt after my death will change into rejoicing and improved lives for family, friends, charities, even people whom I have never met.

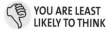 **YOU ARE LEAST LIKELY TO THINK**

That was depressing.

 DON'T

Don't be among the half of all adults in the U.S. who die without having made a will.

WHO SAYS?

When it comes time to die, make sure all you have to do is die.

Jim Elliot, martyred missionary to the Auca tribe of Ecuador, 1927–1956

To Help You Reflect

[Jesus said,] "Be on guard! Be alert! You do not know when that time will come. It's like a man going away: He leaves his house and puts his servants in charge, each with his assigned task, and tells the one at the door to keep watch."

Mark 13:33–34

The saying that is written will come true: "Death has been swallowed up in victory." Where, O death, is your victory? Where, O death, is your sting?

1 Corinthians 15:54–55

The date I made my will:

Where can my copy of it be found?

Who will rejoice because of what I have done?

What I will remember between here and heaven:

20 *Visit an Orthodox service*

How? Visit www.orthodoxinfo.com to learn more about the history, beliefs, and liturgy of Orthodox worship. To find out where you can attend an Orthodox worship service in your area, check your phone book or ask your pastor to help you.

For reasons of security and good etiquette, you should phone ahead and set up an appropriate time to visit. Perhaps this can be something you do as a group with your church family, under the guidance of your pastor.

What Should I Expect?

Before the service, worshipers walk slowly between icons, gazing at them intently, lighting candles in front of or perhaps kissing them. They find a place to stand silently, praying or reading a Bible. The liturgy is almost entirely sung or chanted, with the priest declaring the glory of God and a choir responding in magnificent harmony. The room is charged with spiritual expectation and there is a repeated chant, "Again and again let us pray in peace to the Lord." The majority of the service quotes directly from the Bible. Psalms and the Lord's Prayer are sung, litanies chanted, and passages of the Bible read clearly. In rich, extended praise Jesus (and to a lesser extent, Mary, the Bible, and other saints represented by the icons) are honored.

For most of the service, the priest is partially hidden behind a tall icon screen (iconostasis), glimpsed through an open door amid swirling clouds of incense. This is where bread and wine are consecrated in a setting of veneration and mystery. Later they are brought into the body of the church and reverently placed inside the mouth of each communicant (including baptized children) with a spoon. More bread is distributed at the side of the church. Prayers for the world, and for those who are sick, follow. And finally, the priest removes his vestments and preaches a sermon.

Orthodox spirituality has a deep loyalty to the ancient past, and teachings laid down three hundred years after Jesus still have authority. Orthodox Christians consider themselves to have preserved the beliefs of the very first Christians.

DON'T Don't ask whether someone can sit beside you to explain what is going on—there are no seats! (This rule is waived if you are elderly or unwell.) And don't cause offense by taking Communion unless you are a full member of the Orthodox Church.

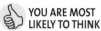

YOU ARE MOST LIKELY TO THINK

I have had a glimpse of the rich and glorious mystery of God's plan for all humankind.

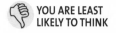

YOU ARE LEAST LIKELY TO THINK

Jesus is my chum.

WHO SAYS?

We should always approach God knowing that we do not know him. We must approach the unsearchable, mysterious God who reveals himself as he chooses; whenever we come to him, we are before a God we do not yet know.

Metropolitan Anthony of Sourozh, head of the Orthodox Church in the UK, 1914–2003

To Help You Reflect

So then, brothers, stand firm and hold to the teachings we passed on to you, whether by word of mouth or by letter. May our Lord Jesus Christ himself and God our Father, who loved us and by his grace gave us eternal encouragement and good hope, encourage your hearts and strengthen you in every good deed and word.

2 Thessalonians 2:15–17

Ascribe to the LORD, O mighty ones,
ascribe to the LORD glory and strength.
Ascribe to the LORD the glory due his name;
worship the LORD in the splendor of his holiness.

Psalm 29:1–2

The date I visited an Orthodox service:

Where was the church?

Adjectives that describe the experience:

What I will remember between here and heaven:

41

21 *Watch a birth*

How? To watch a human birth you must be medically qualified or the person nominated by a mother-to-be as her "birth partner." This can be the father of the baby, or a close friend or relative. Birth partners give vital support and encouragement. There are practical things you can offer too, such as giving a back massage, fetching cool drinks, or being the uncomplaining target of curses!

There are many ways of watching the birth of an animal. For those who live in farming communities or breed dogs it is part of a way of life. Those who live in towns need to make a special effort, and that may involve contacting friends of friends until you reach a hospitable farmer. There are farms open to the public that make a feature of allowing visitors to witness lambs being born in spring. Use your Internet search engine and search "visit a farm" for listings of farms that welcome visitors. Local and state fairs may also provide opportunities to see livestock and meet farmers or those who raise particular animals who would welcome you to watch a live birth. Some museums and zoos exhibit incubators filled with eggs in various stages of hatching. Watching a tiny, wet baby chick peck through its shell and stumble into the open world makes you appreciate the effort it takes just to be born.

What Should I Expect? Watching a birth is an

extremely emotional experience. In all cultures, the fact that something begins as intangible love and ends as flesh and bone is a wonder that inspires awe and joy. Our increased understanding of the science that explains it has not diminished our desire to cry out in thanks to God for something that seems miraculous. So expect to have such a strong sense of involvement that your own body strains in sympathy with the mother, and then to feel exhilarated when the new life has entered the world.

Use the experience as a chance to think about your own place in the world. Enjoy the fact that you are breathing the air of God's world for a purpose, even if it is hard to ascertain. And then offer the new life that has begun, whether it is human, cat, or caterpillar, into the care of the one who has sustained life on this planet for a good reason for so many centuries.

DON'T

Don't assume that children will be fascinated by animals giving birth—they may find it more repulsive than wondrous.

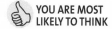 **YOU ARE MOST LIKELY TO THINK**

Birth is a miracle. Life is a miracle. I am a miracle.

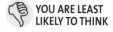 **YOU ARE LEAST LIKELY TO THINK**

Life has no meaning.

To Help You Reflect

You created my inmost being;
you knit me together in my mother's womb.
I praise you because I am fearfully and
    wonderfully made;
your works are wonderful, I know that full
well.

Psalm 139:13–14

[Jesus said,] "A woman giving birth to a child has pain because her time has come; but when her baby is born she forgets the anguish because of her joy that a child is born into the world. So with you: now is your time of grief, but I will see you again and you will rejoice, and no one will take away your joy."

John 16:21–22

The date I watched a birth:

Human or animal?

What circumstances led to me being there?

What I will remember between here and heaven:

22 *Conquer your fear*

How? Everyone is moderately afraid of something (going to the dentist, for instance—odontophobia). Most people struggle through their aversions because they have them in proportion (you can shrug off the anxious moment when an airplane takes off—aviophobia—because the chances of dying in a plane crash are one in 1.5 million). However, for a few people the fear is so intense that it makes life miserable. A fear of eating in public (phagophobia) or of contact with dirt (mysophobia) can so limit what you are able to do that the joy goes out of life.

Start your journey into freedom with a visit to your GP. Your doctor can direct you to an appropriate person or organization that can help you learn coping skills as you seek to overcome your phobia. Visit www.web4health.info/en for information on a variety of phobias.

Even if you do not suffer from a phobia yourself, understanding the dynamics of phobias will give you more compassion and understanding for a loved one or friend who does.

One-to-one behavior therapy is also available privately, and airlines offer one-day courses that effectively address the fear of flying.

What Should I Expect? Beneath varied fears lie the

same roots—anxieties about failure, rejection, or disapproval. There are two steps to dealing with them. The first is to build up your inner strength so that you are better able to cope. The second is to identify and understand your fears, because knowing how and why they are damaging you removes the power they have.

Treatments usually begin by learning techniques that induce calm, such as breathing exercises. Then the process involves being exposed to the things that frighten you in a gradual, structured way. It begins with a gentle encounter with whatever causes your fear in a way in which, with the support of others, you feel quite safe. It then builds in intensity to a point at which you are able to face difficult situations without panic. This is accompanied by conversation, analysis, and (if you are conquering your fear in the company of Christians) prayer.

DON'T

Don't overlook the fact that God has given us the ability to fear for a good reason. Fear of standing on precarious cliff-tops (acrophobia) or walking alone down dark alleys (achluophobia) is entirely sensible.

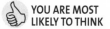 **YOU ARE MOST LIKELY TO THINK**

"Free at last! Free at last! Thank God Almighty, I am free at last."

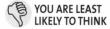 **YOU ARE LEAST LIKELY TO THINK**

I'm planning to develop ecclesiophobia. (It's a fear of going to church.)

WHO SAYS?

To Help You Reflect

God has said, "Never will I leave you; never will I forsake you." So we say with confidence, "The Lord is my helper; I will not be afraid. What can man do to me?"

Hebrews 13:5–6

My son, preserve sound judgment and discernment, do not let them out of your sight; they will be life for you, an ornament to grace your neck. Then you will go on your way in safety, and your foot will not stumble; when you lie down, you will not be afraid; when you lie down, your sleep will be sweet. Have no fear of sudden disaster or of the ruin that overtakes the wicked, for the LORD will be your confidence.

Proverbs 3:21–26

The date I began to tackle my fear:

The name of my fear and the length of time it has trapped me:

Describe the treatment:

What I will remember between here and heaven:

23 *Grapple with Revelation*

How? Revelation is the last book in the Bible. It is difficult to read because it is full of symbolism to which we no longer possess the key. Literature like this is called apocalyptic (Daniel 7—12 and Matthew 24 are other examples). Its characteristic is a vision that God triumphs at the end of a devastating battle against the forces of evil, pictured as fantastical beasts. Its original readers recognized this kind of writing, so the author did not bother to explain it.

Guides include accessible books such as *The Revelation of John* by William Barclay (New Daily Study Bible) to weightier commentaries such as *Revelation* by Brian Blount (New Testament Library). Care should be taken using the Internet to research Revelation, because its mystical content entices many who see in it allusions to events taking place in the world today. A guide that is worth taking seriously comes from a theologian who tells you even-handedly about different ways of interpreting the book, not someone who ingeniously connects "hidden meanings" to produce a crackpot theory that the world will end at midnight.

What Should I Expect? You will discover four major ways of interpreting Revelation. The preterist view understands that every event described by the writer alludes to something that was actually happening in his own day (for example, the evil Babylon refers to Rome, where Christians were being persecuted in the first century). The futurist view sees the book predicting the way the world will end (a view that was popular in the twentieth century, with many books encouraging Christians that faith will take them away from tribulation and straight to heaven when Jesus returns). The historicist view is that the mysterious events symbolize the whole sweep of history from the first century to the future end of the world (Protestants of the sixteenth century popularized this view, using it to attack Roman Catholicism, but they were wrong to presume that they were the last generation who would inhabit this planet, and there is no reason why those who think it today are any wiser). An idealist interpretation is that the writer did not set out to prophesy events, but to inspire Christians to persevere through suffering to the triumphant end.

DON'T

Don't take any
sentence of Revelation
literally, because that
was never the writer's
intention.

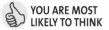 **YOU ARE MOST
LIKELY TO THINK**

I hardly understood a
word, but it's clear that,
because of Jesus, the world
is in safe hands and I'm on
the winning side.

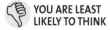 **YOU ARE LEAST
LIKELY TO THINK**

The Norman conquest,
the great Chicago fire, the
moon landings—they are
all predicted here.

WHO SAYS?

The book of Rev-
elation [assures] its
readers that this
world belongs to God
and not to the forces
of evil. Through the
use of vivid and
powerful imagery it
emphasizes that God
will act to put things
right, no matter how
long such action may
seem to be delayed ...
a new world, where
sin, misery and evil
have no further place.

John Drane, theologian

To Help You Reflect

"These words are trustworthy and true....
Blessed is he who keeps the words of the
prophecy in this book.... Worship God!" Then
[the angel] told me, "Do not seal up the words
of the prophecy of this book, because the time
is near." ... He who testifies to these things says,
"Yes, I am coming soon." Amen. Come, LORD Jesus.
Revelation 22:6, 7, 9, 10, 20

Command certain men not to teach false
doctrines any longer nor to devote themselves
to myths and endless genealogies. These
promote controversies rather than God's work—
which is by faith. The goal of this command is
love, which comes from a pure heart and a good
conscience and a sincere faith.
1 Timothy 1:3–5

The date I studied Revelation:

The most important things I discovered:

My hopes and fears for human destiny:

What I will remember between here and heaven:

24 *Be still*

How? This may not be as obvious as it seems. Seek out a time and place where you can be reasonably certain that you will not be disturbed. It will be virtually impossible to find complete silence, but at least try to exclude the noise of music, broadcasting, or chatter.

Set an alarm to go off at the end of the time you have allocated. Seat yourself comfortably. Shut your eyes. See the shapes and colors in the darkness behind your eyelids. Slowly become conscious of your breathing. Use this to help you get in touch with your body and to disclose the level of tension within it. Tense all your muscles, and then relax them one at a time, starting with your toes and progressing to your head, until there is no tension left. Inhale deeply, slowly tilting your head back. Then exhale, allowing your head slowly to rock forward. Do this several times.

Become silent, first outwardly and then inwardly. Pay attention to the fact that God is present. Don't reflect on any particular thing, but let thoughts take you by surprise. Create a space that God can fill with God's love for you.

What Should I Expect? The first thing you will be

aware of is the sound of your breathing. Thank God for something you never usually hear. You may be still enough to hear other unexpected sounds, such as bird song or distant traffic. They may help the process, rather than distracting you, so thank God for another thing you do not often listen to.

Use each breath as a means of centering your thoughts on God. As you exhale, tell God that you are pushing away your anxiety over your job. As you inhale, tell God that you are breathing in his peace. As you exhale, tell God that you are pushing away your frustration about your church. As you inhale, tell God that you are breathing in his faithfulness. If it is possible, let God progressively occupy all your attention. If your mind wanders to something concerning your home or family, make that one of the things you consciously breathe out, and draw in a breath that is full of things you appreciate about God. Then listen once again.

Make the most of the fact that for this period of time, no one has any expectations of you. You and God can simply be at one with each other. At the end, thank God for having been with you.

DON'T

Don't go into the exercise with any specific expectations. If ideas or feelings come, fine. If not, it is also fine. Simply enjoy the absence of noise and activity.

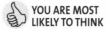 **YOU ARE MOST LIKELY TO THINK**

How is it that ten minutes of boredom feel like ten hours, but ten minutes of silence feel like ten seconds?

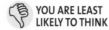 **YOU ARE LEAST LIKELY TO THINK**

Where are the Rolling Stones when you need them?

To Help You Reflect

Because of the LORD's great love we are not consumed,
for his compassions never fail.
They are new every morning; great is your faithfulness.
I say to myself, "The LORD is my portion; therefore I will wait for him."
The LORD is good to those whose hope is in him,
to the one who seeks him;
it is good to wait quietly for the salvation of the LORD.
It is good for a man to bear the yoke while he is young.
Let him sit alone in silence, for the LORD has laid it on him.

Lamentations 3:22–28

Be still, and know that I am God;
I will be exalted among the nations,
I will be exalted in the earth.

Psalm 46:10

The date I sought stillness:

Where?

Adjectives that describe the experience:

What I will remember between here and heaven:

---

25 *Grow something you eat*

How? Make a plan for growing something that fits the circumstances in which you live. If you live in an apartment, germinate sprouts, such as alfalfa or mung beans. It is possible to buy trays for sprouting beans, but any glass bowl can be used, covered, but with holes allowing air in. Soak the seeds overnight in water and drain them. Spread them, remembering that they will increase in size many times over. Keep them in the dark for the first three days, then bring them into the light, adding a small amount of water twice a day. They should be ready to eat, as part of a salad, in seven days.

With even less space, grow cress or mustard, which require only a plate and some paper towels. Sprinkle the seeds, add water, and put the plate in a place that is reasonably warm and light. After five days, add this to egg or cheese sandwiches.

If you have a little space outside, grow herbs in a container at least ten inches wide and deep. Any pot will do, as long as it has holes in the bottom so that it drains (a growbag has a mixture of soil and compost already prepared for you). Try growing parsley, because it can be added to almost anything you cook. In spring, put compost in the container and push the parsley seeds in three-quarters of an inch deep. Pour boiling water over them, and put the pot where it will get a few hours of sunshine every day. Water the seeds on days when it doesn't rain and hope for the best. Four weeks later you should have parsley to cut.

Garlic also grows effortlessly if you pull apart a bulb in October, plant individual cloves three-quarters of an inch deep and four inches apart, and pull them up in June.

What Should I Expect? There are five good reasons for growing something to eat. First and most obvious, fruit and vegetables are good for you. Second, the taste and crispness of such fresh produce greatly exceeds anything you buy in a supermarket. Third, you will know exactly what chemicals have and haven't been added. Fourth, you know that transporting it from where it grew to your plate added nothing to global warming. And finally, you will be part of the day-to-day miracle through which God constantly enriches the planet with life and growth.

DON'T

Don't abandon what you have planted. Water it little and often.

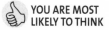 **YOU ARE MOST LIKELY TO THINK**

Our God, who created everything out of nothing, goes on and on making life begin even in the most unpromising circumstances.

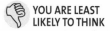 **YOU ARE LEAST LIKELY TO THINK**

The best way to eat is as individuals each sitting in front of our own television.

WHO SAYS?

There is something about the simple tasks of washing, peeling and cooking a carrot, picking herbs and adding them to the pot, growing a spindly tomato plant and eating its fruit, that makes it transparent that in our living we are ordered to a Creator. If we eat at all, and if there is work for our hands to do, it is because [God has provided] it for us.

Clare Watkins, theologian

To Help You Reflect

I know that there is nothing better for men than to be happy and do good while they live. That everyone may eat and drink, and find satisfaction in all his toil—this is the gift of God.

Ecclesiastes 3:12–13

"I will bring back my exiled people Israel,"
    [declares the Lord].
"They will rebuild the ruined cities and live
    in them.
They will plant vineyards and drink their
    wine;
they will make gardens and eat their fruit."

Amos 9:14

The date I first ate something I had grown:

What was it?

The people with whom I ate the meal:

What I will remember between here and heaven:

26 *Blog*

How? A blog (or weblog, to use its full name) is a personal diary made public on the Internet. Web sites such as www .blogger.com provide a structure that allows you to do so simply. As you update it regularly, visitors to your blog can comment on what you have written or e-mail you. You can decide whether you want everyone in the world to be able to read your thoughts, or whether to protect them with a password that you make known only to your friends.

You can use the space as a daily pulpit, a political commentary, a journal of your experiences during an interesting phase of your life, a photo album, a record of what God is teaching you, or a collaborative space in which to discuss ideas. You create a profile that describes the content of your blog so that people who share your interests become aware that you are writing.

When you first visit the Web site that facilitates this, you will be asked to create an account by supplying your name and e-mail address. You can choose a color, name, and layout so that your blog looks distinctive. Then you are ready to post your first entry. Send the URL (the Internet address at which to find your blog) to anyone whom you hope might be interested in reading it, and publicize it by adding it to business cards, e-mails, Christmas cards, or anywhere that will encourage readers to access it (which will in turn encourage you to keep writing).

What Should I Expect?
The value of blogging is not only that you can communicate with others, but also that you can organize your own thoughts about what is happening to you and to the world. Keep your posts interesting so that reading them is a pleasure, not a chore. (Your trip to the supermarket is not interesting; your decision to avoid going to supermarkets for a month is!)

You will find yourself looking at what you do through other people's eyes. This will make you increasingly aware that what you do and write are witnesses to your Christian beliefs. The number of people visiting your site will be small at the beginning, but it will grow, and so will your opportunity to influence society for good.

DON'T

 **YOU ARE MOST LIKELY TO THINK**

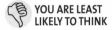 **YOU ARE LEAST LIKELY TO THINK**

Don't publish anything about the failings or illnesses of friends or family that would be upsetting for them to read in a public forum.

The things God is teaching me about being alive are important, and this is a way of sharing them.

I am getting blogged down in this!

WHO SAYS?

I do hope blogging becomes a tool that Christians embrace and learn to wield effectively. It's a great way to be in the culture and comment on it. It's also a great way to sharpen up your own ability to think about the arguments of others and make your own rhetoric more effective. . . . Our blogs should be well-written, interesting and demonstrate a decent level of thought and reasoning power. There are plenty of Christians out there who can and should start up a blog and get in the game.

Martin Roth, Australian commentator and blogger

To Help You Reflect

May the words of my mouth and the meditation of my heart be pleasing in your sight, O LORD, my Rock and my Redeemer. Psalm 19:14

The date I began my blog:

The URL:

What I have written about so far:

What I will remember between here and heaven:

27 *Write a letter to your future self*

How? Search through your desk and find a piece of paper or a blank card that you tucked away for a rainy day. Or purchase a note card or sheet of stationery that appeals to you.

Set a time when you will not be interrupted for at least an hour. Turn off the computer and cell phone, and fix yourself a cup of tea. Play some soothing background music. Choose a pen that feels comfortable in your hand and inspires you to write.

First, write the date on the top of the page, including the day of the week. Write down the time. Then address the letter as you would to someone very dear to you—but make that person yourself.

Write down what is going on in your life. What makes you happy? What concerns do you have? Who are the people who bless you? What are your dreams for the future? What would you like to be doing a year from now?

Include some thoughts and reflections on your faith journey. What questions of faith are you having right now? Is there a problem you need to turn over to God? How do you plan to nurture your faith in the coming year?

When you are finished, let the letter sit for a day before sealing it. Address the envelope with your own name. Write "open on" and date it a year from now.

Tuck the letter in a drawer, where you will see it on occasion but not every day. Or put the letter in your safe deposit box at the bank. Or, address the envelope and give it to a trusted friend, and ask that person to mail it to you in one year.

If you forget about the letter and don't come across it for several years, that's okay. One day you will find it, and the contents will be just as cherished no matter when you read them.

What Should I Expect? Expect to be surprised when a letter arrives in the mail addressed to you in a handwriting that you recognize but don't quite place right away. You may be a bit anxious trying to remember what you wrote a year ago. More likely, you will feel excitement at receiving a letter you had forgotten all about. When you read your own words to your future self, you will be amazed at the ways you felt when you wrote the letter. You'll be glad you took the time to put your thoughts and dreams on paper.

DON'T

Don't criticize your penmanship, your choice of words, or what you wrote. Remember, it was written from your heart.

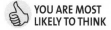 **YOU ARE MOST LIKELY TO THINK**

I'm really glad to hear from myself!

YOU ARE LEAST LIKELY TO THINK

I'm not a very good writer.

To Help You Reflect

So from the beginning I have been convinced of all this
and have thought it out and left it in writing:
All the works of the LORD are good,
and he will supply every need in its time.
No one can say, "This is not as good as that,"
for everything proves good in its appointed time.
So now sing praise with all your heart and voice,
and bless the name of the LORD.

Ecclesiastes 39:32–35 NRSV

See what large letters I use as I write to you with my own hand!

Galatians 6:11

The date I wrote a letter to myself:

Where I put the letter for safekeeping:

How I felt writing the letter:

What I will remember between here and heaven:

28 *Have a conversation with the preacher*

How? "Sermon" originally meant discourse or conversation, and the sermons of the early church may have been closer to dialogues in which ideas, Scripture, and the experience of having known Jesus came together in order to pursue the truth.

Has a recent sermon piqued your interest? Ask the preacher for an opportunity to discuss how he or she reached particular conclusions, and inquire how the preacher prefers to discuss such things—in person, or by letter, e-mail, or telephone. Call the church office in advance and set up a time and place to meet.

Prepare some questions in advance about a particular sermon or maybe a theological topic. If you give the preacher a heads-up about what you want to discuss, that alleviates the preacher's concern about your reasons for scheduling a conversation.

Be open to having different opinions on a topic. Having a healthy conversation does not mean that two people have to agree on every point. There is a freedom in recognizing that you can disagree with someone and not take it personally.

Preachers may get more feedback when they say something that irritates or upsets someone, and not much when the sermon really hits the target or is appreciated. Let your preacher know when a sermon has spoken in a good way to you or challenged you in an area where you needed to be challenged. Preachers need good feedback as well as constructive criticism.

What Should I Expect?
Most preachers will be glad to have a chance to converse outside the restrictions of Sunday morning. Getting together for a cup of tea or coffee can be a nice break for a preacher in the midst of all the paperwork and planning that also goes into worship preparations.

The goal of the meeting should be that both you and the preacher end up affirming the various ways each of you honor God in your words and your work.

Another possible outcome is the formation of a discussion group that includes the preacher and others who want to discuss thoughts and issues raised by the sermons.

Expect the preacher to offer to pray with you, and return the favor if you feel confident enough to do so. Those who regularly pray for others welcome the chance to have someone pray for them.

DON'T

Don't challenge the speaker immediately after he or she has preached (an extremely vulnerable time). Wait a couple of days to make contact.

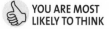 **YOU ARE MOST LIKELY TO THINK**

The truth (even when it is awkward, elusive, or bruising) is always worth pursuing.

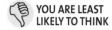 **YOU ARE LEAST LIKELY TO THINK**

I love telling people how wrong they are.

WHO SAYS?

It is the worst trial of a preacher's life that he is ever set up on a pedestal, where he himself is seen in a false perspective, and may easily come to see himself as others see him. Still, he does want encouragement sometimes, poor thing! And an honest, loving friend, who blames as well as praises, can give it.

Herbert Hensley Henson, bishop of Durham, 1863–1947

To Help You Reflect

[In Ephesus, Paul] took the disciples with him and had discussions daily in the lecture hall of Tyrannus. This went on for two years, so that all the Jews and Greeks who lived in the province of Asia heard the word of the LORD.

Acts 19:9–10

Don't have anything to do with foolish and stupid arguments, because you know they produce quarrels. And the LORD's servant must not quarrel; instead, he must be kind to everyone, able to teach, not resentful. Those who oppose him he must gently instruct, in the hope that God will grant them repentance leading them to a knowledge of the truth.

2 Timothy 2:23–25

The date I spoke with the preacher:

This is what I asked about:

The tone of our conversation was . . .

What I will remember between here and heaven:

29 _Write a hymn_

How? If you are an experienced musician, you will already have a sense of how a phrase and melody might emerge alongside each other, even if you have never attempted it. This activity is more challenging if you do not play an instrument, which is a good reason to attempt it. Choose an established melody (perhaps a hymn tune or a folk song) and create new words for it. The psalms of the Bible are inexhaustible sources of inspiration, expressing a range of emotions and questions that men and women have addressed to God in every subsequent century. Try to rephrase a line from a psalm in a way that fits naturally into the rhythm of one of the lines of the tune. If it stays in your mind, extend the theme into a verse, and then several. Follow the rhyming pattern of the song's original words.

The Calvin Institute of Christian Worship (see the Web site at www.calvin.edu/worship/stories/hymn_writing.php) gives a wonderful background on the history and purpose of hymn writing plus a link to a Web site of "tips for beginning hymn writers" by Carl P. Daw Jr., an Episcopal priest and the author of many hymns.

What Should I Expect? Write from your heart,
expressing concepts that you genuinely feel. The words might state what God is like, or they might be a personal response to God written in the first person. Praise is central to worship, but there is also an important place for hymns that are prayers for justice, statements of commitment, or pleas for forgiveness. Match the nature of the words to the mood of the chosen music.

Be strict with yourself and avoid anything that is too obvious, rhymes that clunk, or lines that need to be sung in an unnatural way to fit the tune. When you have finished, use the song as your own act of worship to God. The main point of composing is to bring joy to God. Show it to friends who are theologically informed or musically talented and ask for their reaction. If they suggest that the hymn would allow others to worship in an uplifting way, explore the possibility of using it at a church. Be ready to revise it after you hear what it sounds like when many people sing it together.

DON'T

Don't waste time looking for a rhyme for "God." Anything you try will cause an unintentional laugh.

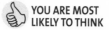
YOU ARE MOST LIKELY TO THINK

Dear Lord and Father of
  mankind,
Forgive our whining ways,
We criticize and can't
  abide
All hymns composed since
  Wesley died,
Revitalize our praise,
Revitalize our praise.

YOU ARE LEAST LIKELY TO THINK

All people that on earth
  do dwell,
Sing my new hymn with
  cheesy voice,
I am tone deaf and cannot
  spell,
But it's a one-off, so rejoice!

To Help You Reflect

Speak to one another with psalms, hymns and spiritual songs. Sing and make music in your heart to the LORD, always giving thanks to God the Father for everything.

Ephesians 5:19–20

Sing to the LORD a new song;
sing to the LORD, all the earth.
Sing to the LORD, praise his name;
proclaim his salvation day after day.
Declare his glory among the nations,
his marvelous deeds among all peoples.
For great is the LORD and most worthy of praise.

Psalm 96:1–4

The date I wrote a hymn:

Its title and its best line:

Has it been sung as an act of worship? If so, where and when?

What I will remember between here and heaven:

30 *Experience the taste of tea*

How? The sipping of tea has come into fashion in the United States, because of both its health benefits and the abundance of specialty coffee and tea shops. Stroll the aisle at the supermarket and you might be amazed at the types of teas available: black, green, white, red, oolong. (Herbal teas are fruit or herbs, and do not contain actual tea leaves, but you can count them as teas.)

Loose tea, tea bags, sachets—teas come in lots of different packaging. Loose tea leaves can be brewed using an infuser, a small mesh basket that fits in your teapot. Tea bags or sachets have the advantage of the leaves being contained, but some people think that the crowding of the leaves diminishes the fullness of the flavor.

To make a delicious pot of tea, fill your teapot with hot water to warm it. Bring a kettle of water to a near boil. Dump the preliminary water in the teapot, add the infuser or tea bag, and pour the nearly boiling water into the pot.

Teas have different brewing guidelines. White teas are meant to steep only a minute, while black teas take longer.

Don't let tea brew too long as a way of making it stronger—the result will be bitter instead. To alter the strength of the tea, vary the amount of leaves or bags you use.

Add sugar, honey, or another sweetener; lemon; mint; milk or cream; or leave the tea as is.

Once you've brewed your tea, sit down in a quiet place, read your favorite Scripture passage, and pray leisurely. Like a good cup of tea, prayer is meant to be savored.

What Should I Expect? Tea drinking is more than just a way of satisfying your thirst. Sipping a properly brewed cup of tea, served in a special cup, by yourself or with a friend, is calming and enlightening. Engage more than your sense of taste. Admire the color of the tea. A black tea might have a golden tint, while a red tea has a deep, rich hue. Inhale the aroma. Is it sweet, pungent, smoky? Feel the warmth of the teacup in your hand. Close your eyes and appreciate the calm sense of sipping a cup of tea without being in a rush to finish.

DON'T

Don't give up if you don't like tea the first time you try it. There are so many different types, one is bound to hit the spot.

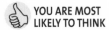 **YOU ARE MOST LIKELY TO THINK**

I've really been missing something all these years!

 **YOU ARE LEAST LIKELY TO THINK**

Tea is for sissies.

To Help You Reflect

As Jesus and his disciples were on their way, he came to a village where a woman named Martha opened her home to him. She had a sister called Mary, who sat at the Lord's feet listening to what he said. But Martha was distracted by all the preparations that had to be made. She came to him and asked, "Lord, don't you care that my sister has left me to do the work by myself? Tell her to help me!" "Martha, Martha," the Lord answered, "you are worried and upset about many things, but only one thing is needed. Mary has chosen what is better, and it will not be taken away from her."

Luke 10:38–42

The date I tried a new variety of tea:

Describe the flavor:

What I would suggest to someone trying tea for the first time:

What I will remember between here and heaven:

31 *Keep a Sabbath*

How? On your calendar, look up the next four Sundays (or, if that is unrealistic, another regular day of the week) and write "special" in the space. Make plans that will allow these to become the most enjoyable and relaxing days of the seven that make up each week.

First, decide what will definitely not happen on those days (for instance, household chores, inadequate sleep, trudging through the supermarket).

Second, decide what you will do instead. Include things that you will recognize as a treat from God to you, and also things that are, in a sense, a treat from you to God. Follow the biblical principles of a Sabbath by including space for worship, space for reflecting on life, and space for administering care to others.

After four Sabbaths, analyze whether this is improving the rhythm of your life and consider extending it. If habits you have got into make the day arduous (such as obligations to cook a special dinner), think creatively about alternatives.

What Should I Expect? At a low point of their
history the Hebrew people were enslaved—no rest, no day off, no care, just the misery of having one's life used as a commodity to achieve wealth for someone else. After they were freed from oppression, they were commanded never to forget what they had been through and never to replicate it when they became the employers rather than the enslaved. There was to be a Sabbath, one day in seven and one year in seven, that was different. The people rested, the land rested, the livestock rested.

God has always been concerned that human life should have a healthy rhythm. He offers a Sabbath day, once in every seven, not because he wants us to do something awkward to please him, but as a gift that will improve our lives. It is a gift to individuals for refreshment and to society so that once in a while the pressure relents.

To keep a Sabbath in this generation involves being strong enough to resist the 24/7 nature of the culture. However, nothing about the day should make it burdensome. Expect to feel invigorated by spending one day completely unlike the way you spend the others.

DON'T

Don't shrug this off if shift work or circumstances mean that it is impossible to treat Sunday as a Sabbath. Nominate another day to keep special instead.

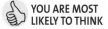 **YOU ARE MOST LIKELY TO THINK**

This has rescued me from the remorseless stream of weekdays that stretch from New Year's Day to Christmas Eve.

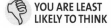 **YOU ARE LEAST LIKELY TO THINK**

I can't wait for the alarm to go off on Monday morning.

To Help You Reflect

For six years you shall sow your land and gather in its yield; but the seventh year you shall let it rest and lie fallow, so that the poor of your people may eat; and what they leave the wild animals may eat ... Six days you shall do your work, but on the seventh day you shall rest, so that your ox and your donkey may have relief, and your homeborn slave and the resident alien may be refreshed.

Exodus 23:10–12 NRSV

There remains, then, a Sabbath-rest for the people of God; for anyone who enters God's rest also rests from his own work, just as God did from his. Let us, therefore, make every effort to enter that rest, so that no one will fall.

Hebrews 4:9–11

The date I began to observe a Sabbath:

The things I decided not to do:

The things I did instead:

What I will remember between here and heaven:

32 *Label your photographs*

How? Choose a method of organizing your collection. A chronological scheme is best for photographs you have taken, but if you have inherited an unlabeled collection from decades past it may be easier to group them by people or events. If you discover photographs whose subject or date are unknown, *Uncovering Your Ancestry through Family Photographs*, by Maureen Taylor, has advice about using clues in the image to track down dates, locations, and (through the help of relatives) names and relationships. The clues include clothing, wedding rings, body language, and even the nature of the stock on which the image is printed.

To ensure that the information is never separated from the images, write directly on the back of the photograph with a No. 2 pencil (not a ball-point pen that will indent the print, nor ink that contains acid). Record the names, the location, the approximate date, and what is taking place. Avoid using self-adhesive labels or tape, because the acid in them irreversibly damages the photos.

What Should I Expect?

The people of God during the centuries recorded in the Old Testament had a burning desire that they should not be forgotten by future generations. They passed on family stories to their children, and instructed them to do the same. And they left physical reminders, like standing stones beside a river, so that the memory of important moments would be indelible.

Photography has made passing on such stories so easy that we take it for granted, but labeling photographs means that the landmarks of your family history can be recorded before it is too late. As you do it, take the opportunity to sit down with your immediate family and explore the photographs. Laugh and cry over the story of how God led you to where you are now, and the people who shared the route. As well as celebrating happy moments, be honest about times when it went wrong, and how God picked you up and pushed you, reluctant and protesting, or maybe loving and obeying, toward the present. Then take and label another photo so that today becomes part of the ongoing story of the journey you are on.

DON'T

Don't leave photographs that are stored in your computer out of the process.

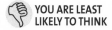 **YOU ARE MOST LIKELY TO THINK**

How did we persuade ourselves that those fashions looked good?

YOU ARE LEAST LIKELY TO THINK

These people should be forgotten.

To Help You Reflect

When the whole nation had finished crossing the Jordan, the LORD said to Joshua, "Choose twelve men from among the people, one from each tribe, and tell them to take up twelve stones from the middle of the Jordan . . . and put them down at the place where you stay tonight. . . . In the future, when your children ask you, 'What do these stones mean?' tell them that the flow of the Jordan was cut off before the ark of the covenant of the LORD. When it crossed the Jordan, the waters of the Jordan were cut off. These stones are to be a memorial to the people of Israel forever." . . . And they are there to this day.

Joshua 4:1–3, 6–7, 9

I constantly remember you in my prayers. . . . I have been reminded of your sincere faith, which first lived in your grandmother Lois and in your mother Eunice and, I am persuaded, now lives in you also. For this reason I remind you to fan into flame the gift of God.

2 Timothy 1:3–6

The date I labeled my photographs:

A person or place I had forgotten was photographed:

A photograph that recalls something that I treasure:

What I will remember between here and heaven:

33 Plan a trip around the world

How? In 1873, when Jules Verne's novel *Around the World in 80 Days* was first published, the thought of globe-trotting in such a length of time seemed remarkable.

Although travel options have shortened the distance between states, countries, and continents, few people are fortunate enough (or have enough fortune) to travel around the world. Don't let that stop you. You can "travel" without leaving home and hardly spend a dime.

Begin with your starting point, which will also be your end point (that part was easy!).

Decide where you will go next, how you will get there, and how much time it will take. For instance, if you start in Chicago and your first major stop is Iceland, will you drive from the Windy City to the Big Apple and fly from there? Or take a train trip through the Northeast and catch a plane in Newfoundland?

Have fun brainstorming the possibilities. Make a list of all the countries you'd like to visit. Consider the transportation options: airline, train, bus, auto.

Once you've narrowed down where you want to go, and how you wish to travel, research airports, plane and train schedules. Visit a travel agent or other place where you can pick up maps and travel brochures (if you're a member of AAA, your membership should include maps and travel aids). Research the history and landmarks of the countries you plan to "visit."

Buy a travel journal and keep track of where you've "been" and how you got there. What sights did you "see"? What foods did you "eat"? How long did you spend in each place? Keep track of mileage and other expenses. That way, at the end of your travels, you'll see how much you saved staying home—or you may decide you really want to see Paris in the spring and find a way to make that dream come true.

What Should I Expect? Planning an imaginary trip around the world can help you figure out where you would like to go for a dream trip someday. You might be motivated to start a travel fund. Or you may realize that you're just as happy traveling from the comfort of your own home. As Dorothy says in the *Wizard of Oz*, "There's no place like home!"

! **DON'T** Don't become a couch potato just because you will never get to all the places you want to go. Explore your neighborhood, city, or state. There's plenty to see and do anywhere.

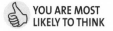

YOU ARE MOST LIKELY TO THINK

There are so many options!

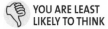

YOU ARE LEAST LIKELY TO THINK

There are so few places I want to go.

WHO SAYS?

One's destination is never a place, but a new way of seeing things.
Henry Miller, American writer

To Help You Reflect

Your statutes have been my songs wherever I make my home.
Psalm 119:54 NRSV

The date I began to plan my trip:

The country that most fascinated me:

How many miles I traveled:

What I will remember between here and heaven:

34 *Create a memorial*

How? The many ways to create a lasting memorial to someone who has died include the following three.

Create a memorial on the Internet. Some memorial Web sites are rather sentimental, but www.relativesremembered.com allows you to post a photograph, write a celebration of someone's life, and, if it is someone known personally to you, e-mail friends to direct their attention to the site.

Some park districts will allow you to donate a memorial bench or garden with a plaque identifying the individual being remembered. Cemeteries may offer this type of tribute as well. It is soothing to sit on a bench given to honor a loved one, while gazing out over the serenity of a park, garden, or beautifully landscaped cemetery.

You can check with your city hall to find out about other ways to create a lasting public memorial for someone.

What Should I Expect?

There are six billion people alive on the planet—that is more than have ever previously lived in its history. The living outnumber the dead. People of previous generations, especially those who had a Christian faith, wanted to be measured by their souls. For their loved ones, the assurance of meeting again in eternal life was a sufficient memorial. However, society in this generation is shaped less by the certainty of resurrection, and for both secular and Christian people the need to remember someone in a distinctive way has become more important.

Creating a memorial gives you the opportunity to reflect on and take joy in the things that were unique about a person, whether it is someone famous or a friend. Working out why and where a person should be remembered involves focusing on the reasons the world is a better place because he or she has been in it. Take time to notice the names on plaques, and register that someone wanted to introduce those people to you. Creating a memorial announces to passers by a deep Christian truth—that life (every life) is worth living.

DON'T

Don't be afraid to suggest to another person that you'd like to memorialize their loved one. It's important for all of us that those we love be remembered.

WHO SAYS?

Reader, if you seek a memorial, look around you.

Christopher Wren, inscribed in St Paul's Cathedral, London, of which he was the architect, 1632–1723

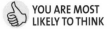
YOU ARE MOST LIKELY TO THINK

When I meet this person in eternal life I will delight to tell them what I have done.

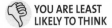
YOU ARE LEAST LIKELY TO THINK

I am not worth remembering.

To Help You Reflect

The LORD says: "To [those] . . . who choose what pleases me and hold fast to my covenant—to them I will give within my temple and its walls a memorial and a name better than sons and daughters; I will give them an everlasting name that will not be cut off."

Isaiah 56:4–5

Let us now sing the praises of famous men,
our ancestors in their generations. . . .
Some of them have left behind a name,
so that others declare their praise.
But of others there is no memory;
they have perished as though they had never
existed. . . .
But these also were godly men,
whose righteous deeds have not been forgotten. . . .
The assembly declares their wisdom,
and the congregation proclaims their praise.

Ecclesiastes 44:1, 8–10, 15 NRSV

The date I succeeded in creating a memorial:

To whom, and where is it?

This is why I want the person to be remembered:

What I will remember between here and heaven:

35 *Join a discussion group*

How? Many churches have discussion groups, meeting either weekly throughout the year or with members of other churches during a particular season (for example, Lent). Approach the leader of your local church and ask what is available. Explain what you are looking for—either a group from diverse backgrounds and ages (to sharpen your mind), or one of people at similar life stages (to share support). If all else fails, offer to start one.

There are published courses that encourage discussion about Christian experience, some requiring only the leader to have a copy, and others requiring every group member to write in their own. They are not essential, but they offer a structure. A good one will have introductory activities that put group members at their ease, Bible passages to read, questions that help you explore the Bible together, opportunities to share experience so that principles of the Christian faith become rooted in everyday life, and ideas that capture the group's imagination and lead to prayer.

The Thoughtful Christian (http://www.thethoughtfulchristian .com) is a Web-based resource center sponsored by the Presbyterian Church (U.S.A.) but is ecumenical in content. The format of the material lends itself to discussion groups of all sizes. Topics are varied and abundant, with studies on the Bible, contemporary issues, world religions, Christian life, and much more. Both Leader's Guides and Participant Handouts are available. Check out the Web site for fees and guidelines.

What Should I Expect? A good discussion group
(which usually means a good discussion group leader) allows you to expand your understanding of God by hearing God described in ways you haven't previously thought of. And it allows you to improve your life by hearing the stories of Christians who have had different experiences from you, and to be encouraged by their faithfulness and strengthened by what they have learned.

Don't feel compelled to say something about every subject, but also don't arrive home feeling frustrated that your opinion went unheard. Listen, even when you disagree. Be aware that, through the voices and opinions of others, God may be speaking to you. And remember that God will teach you as much through the relationships that grow as through the ideas you discuss.

DON'T Don't forget that not all discussion groups have Christian subjects or members. A book club, meeting to discuss novels, is also a place where your understanding of God and life will grow if you allow it to. So is a local political party or a philosophy class.

 YOU ARE MOST LIKELY TO THINK

We are more likely to understand God together than we are as individuals.

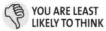 **YOU ARE LEAST LIKELY TO THINK**

I have so much to teach the others.

WHO SAYS?

"Teaching that begins with questions is both a moral and a pedagogical choice. A teacher teaches with questions because she or he believes that it is a better way to teach, and a better way to be a teacher. Yet to succeed at this, the questions must be real questions: questions that puzzle, confuse, and interest."
Nicholas C. Burbles, Educator

To Help You Reflect

The brothers sent Paul and Silas away to Berea. On arriving there, they went to the Jewish synagogue. Now the Bereans . . . received the message with great eagerness and examined the Scriptures every day to see if what Paul said was true.

Acts 17:10–11

[In Ephesus] Paul . . . took the disciples with him and had discussions daily in the lecture hall of Tyrannus. This went on for two years, so that all the Jews and Greeks who lived in the province of Asia heard the word of the LORD.

Acts 19:9–10

The date I joined a discussion group:

The subject under discussion:

The most interesting thing that was said:

What I will remember between here and heaven:

36 *Go Christmas caroling*

How? Chestnuts roasting on an open fire are not something most people experience during the holiday season, but it does conjure up some nice, sentimental images. Yuletide carols being sung by a choir—that's more likely.

There's been a resurgence in a lot of churches of singing only Advent carols during Advent, and saving the Christmas carols until Christmas Day. But let's face it, singing Christmas carols is one of the joys of the season. And even though it is liturgically appropriate to wait until December 25 to sing "Away in a Manger" and "Joy to the World," having a good excuse to sing our favorite carols earlier in December isn't such a bad thing.

Talk to your pastor about organizing a group to go caroling at a senior care facility. Get a list of folks in your congregation who are unable to get out of their homes due to health or other issues. Call these people in advance and let them know when you will be coming by, so they can be prepared and enjoy the anticipation of a visit. Bake cookies and prepare plates of home-baked goodies to deliver to the people you visit.

Invite people of all ages to participate. About forty minutes before you intend to start your trek, gather carolers at a designated site (maybe the church?) for a brief "rehearsal." Have booklets of music and words for every singer. If you are driving, make sure all the drivers have maps with routes marked clearly. Divide into teams and off you go!

Afterward, gather at the church or in someone's home and share stories of those you met and how it felt to sing carols to people who might not be able to get to church for Christmas. Feast on cookies and hot chocolate and maybe even try roasting those chestnuts!

What Should I Expect? It won't be a surprise for you to discover that you feel doubly blessed: blessed by giving and blessed by receiving. The gratitude from those to whom you sing and the company of old and new friends will warm your heart and spirit even better than that hot chocolate you share at the end of your caroling. Expect to put this event on your calendar next year, and the year after that, and ... why not just go ahead now and plan to make this an annual event?

DON'T

Don't think you have to have a great voice. Sing with a joyful heart, and the Spirit will provide the harmony.

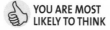 **YOU ARE MOST LIKELY TO THINK**

Christ was in our midst today.

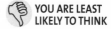 **YOU ARE LEAST LIKELY TO THINK**

I would rather have stayed home and watched football.

WHO SAYS?

The earth has grown old with its
    burden of care
But at Christmas it always is
    young,
The heart of the jewel burns
    lustrous and fair
And its soul full of music breaks
    the air,
When the song of angels is sung.
        Phillips Brooks, clergyman
        and author

To Help You Reflect

Sing to the LORD, all the earth;
    Proclaim his salvation day after day.
            1 Chronicles 16:23

The date I went Christmas caroling:

One person or family I got to meet:

The most requested Christmas carol:

What I will remember between here and heaven:

37 *Learn to sign*

How? About 20 million people in the United States have some degree of hearing difficulty. It is nearly impossible, however, to have an accurate estimate, since those who are legally deaf have not been counted in the U.S. Census since 1930 (see www .Gallaudet.edu/deaf-faq-stats-us.shtml for an explanation of the problems with garnering statistics on the deaf population).

American Sign Language (ASL) is the dominant form of sign language in most of the English-speaking parts of North America. It is used in other countries as well.

Children can learn to sign earlier than they can learn to speak. Many parents of children with unimpaired hearing teach their children basic signs to indicate hunger, thirst, sleep. Churches teach songs to children using some sign language. The signs for various Christian words can add a wonderful depth of meaning to the "hearing" of God's Word. The word for "Jesus," for instance, incorporates touching the palm on each hand, reminding us of the wounds Christ suffered from crucifixion.

To find a place in your area where you can take a class in American Sign Language, call a local college. Even if a class is not offered there, you may be able to find the information you need.

What Should I Expect? Deafness is a cruel disability because it is hidden, and the difficulties of those who have hearing impediments are sometimes mistaken for a lack of intelligence. Entering witty, intellectual, or gossipy conversation by signing dispels that very quickly. ASL is a language with its own beauty, slang, and regional variations, just like Italian or Welsh. Its logic makes the vocabulary memorable, but it has a grammar distinct from spoken English. The sight of a church full of people enthusiastically praising God with every part of their bodies, but not one spoken word, is inspirational.

The visual nature of signing lends itself beautifully to conversations about everyday life, but there are fewer signs for the abstract theological words that sometimes feature in the way Christians talk. This means that discussions about God have to avoid clichés and be rephrased in more literal ways. Communicating in ASL can clarify some of the obscurities of the language we use in worship. It really is the Word made flesh.

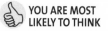

DON'T Don't impose conversation on a deaf person if you are able to hear. Most deaf clubs welcome hearing people, but the custom is for deaf people to invite hearing people into their signed conversation, not the other way round.

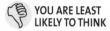

YOU ARE MOST LIKELY TO THINK

Beyond sound, there are millions of ways in which God is communicating. Now that I have encountered one more of them I see God clearer.

YOU ARE LEAST LIKELY TO THINK

I give up. I'll just shout.

WHO SAYS?

The problem is not that [deaf people] do not hear. The problem is that the hearing world does not listen.

Jesse Jackson, American church leader and politician

To Help You Reflect

"Bring my sons from afar
and my daughters from the ends of the earth—
everyone who is called by my name,
whom I created for my glory, whom I formed and
    made.
Lead out those who have eyes but are blind,
who have ears but are deaf. . . .
You are my witnesses," declares the LORD,
"and my servant whom I have chosen,
so that you may know and believe me."

Isaiah 43:6–8, 10

Jesus commanded them not to tell anyone [about his miracles]. But the more he did so, the more they kept talking about it. People were overwhelmed with amazement. "He has done everything well," they said. "He even makes the deaf hear and the mute speak." Mark 7:36–37

The date I gained a qualification in ASL:

My favorite word or phrase to sign:

Names of some deaf people with whom I have had conversations:

What I will remember between here and heaven:

38 Make a family tree

How? Do you know the name of your great-great-grandmother? The date of your grandfather's birth? It is shocking how quickly this information gets lost with the passing of time.

You may be fortunate enough to have a family Bible with a record of your family's dates of births, weddings, and deaths. If you have access to your family history, make sure it gets passed along to others in the family so it doesn't get lost.

The Internet makes it easier to track down genealogical information. Software is available that helps you organize family history. The National Archives has a helpful Web site (www .archives.gov/genealogy) that is great for beginners seeking information on their genealogy and includes links to other sites.

Go one step further than just recording names and dates; learn the stories that have shaped your history. Do you have family members who remember the Great Depression? Ask them to share their memories of those days. Set up interviews in person or by phone. Write down the stories and make a collection. Give these anthologies as gifts to your children and grandchildren. Keep adding chapters.

Some questions you might ask: What home do you remember from your childhood? What were your favorite foods? What were your holiday traditions? How old were you when you attended your first funeral, and whose was it?

Include a family faith history. Track down the dates of your family's baptisms. Is there a baptismal gown that has been passed down through the generations? What church denominations are part of your history? What do people remember about growing up in church?

If you are adopted, you can trace the history of your adopted family as well as your birth family, if you and your loved ones are comfortable with this. Remember, "family" is a broad term and doesn't refer only to blood relatives.

What Should I Expect? Researching your genealogy
can start as an interest and turn into a hobby. There are clubs and organizations for people who seek to go back in their family history. This can be addictive! Even if you're satisfied going back only a generation or two, know that the history you've gathered will be treasured by generations yet to come.

DON'T

Don't keep the information to yourself. Share it with others in the family, and keep a copy in your safe deposit box.

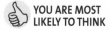 **YOU ARE MOST LIKELY TO THINK**

Everybody's life is interesting and of worth.

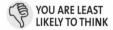 **YOU ARE LEAST LIKELY TO THINK**

My place in the world does not matter.

WHO SAYS?

Parents can only give good advice or put them on the right paths, but the final forming of a person's character lies in their own hands.

Anne Frank, diarist and Holocaust victim

To Help You Reflect

For this reason I kneel before the Father, from whom his whole family in heaven and on earth derives its name. I pray that out of his glorious riches he may strengthen you with power through his Spirit in your inner being, so that Christ may dwell in your hearts through faith.

Ephesians 3:14–17

My favorite memory:

Where I keep my family history:

What I learned about my family that I did not know before:

What I will remember between here and heaven:

39 *Gaze at the night sky*

How? All you need are your eyes and a dark, cloudless sky. However, a chart or planisphere (a map with a moving part that reveals the changing appearance of the night sky) will increase your appreciation. In recent years, streetlights and illuminated buildings have dramatically reduced the visibility of the night sky from towns, so try to find an isolated (but safe) place.

The moon, with its shape appearing to change as the earth's shadow crosses it, is the most obvious feature. Star patterns, or constellations, that have legendary names such as Orion and Cassiopeia can be identified by picking out the more vivid stars among the millions of others. With the help of a star chart it is possible to identify the brighter planets that orbit our own sun.

At different times of the year, and at different latitudes, the appearance of the sky changes (for instance, a full moon that in the Northern Hemisphere has the appearance of a face seems to show a silhouette of a rabbit from the Southern Hemisphere). Basic information about astronomy to enhance the experience can be found by visiting www.astronomy.com.

What Should I Expect? Let your mind get lost in

the impossible task of imagining the size of God's creation, as you consider the distance between you and the dots of light you can see. Then consider the detail of God's work—each star a sun around which planets circle, orbited by their own moons, of which God has detailed knowledge. As a sense of awe opens up within you, direct toward God the warmth you feel at being part of such a complex cosmos.

Go on to think about your place in God's creation. On planets millions of light-years away, suns are rising and setting in majestic colors with no one to see them. Lucky you to have been created a human, able to appreciate beauty and wonder! The same God who is working on such a vast scale is intricately interested in the detail of your life. That is the measure of God's love. Nothing you could say, sing, or think comes close to expressing the greatness of God, but try your best anyway!

DON'T

Don't use an ordinary flashlight because it will impair what you can see in the sky. Instead, adapt one by wrapping red tissue paper or cellophane over the light.

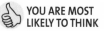 **YOU ARE MOST LIKELY TO THINK**

The time and scale of the project on which God is at work is breathtaking.

 **YOU ARE LEAST LIKELY TO THINK**

The most important thing that has ever happened to the cosmos is me.

WHO SAYS?

Question the beautiful earth, question the beautiful sea, question the beautiful air, amply spread everywhere. Question the beautiful sky, question the constellations of stars, question the sun making the day glorious with its brightness, question the moon tempering the darkness of the following night with its splendor.... They all answer you, "Take a look! We are beautiful." Their beauty is their witness. Who made these beautiful, changeable things, if not the Great Unchanging Beauty?

Augustine, bishop of Hippo, 354–430

To Help You Reflect

When I consider your heavens,
the work of your fingers,
the moon and the stars,
which you have set in place,
what is man that you are
  mindful of him,
the son of man that you care for
  him?
You made him a little lower than
  the heavenly beings
and crowned him with glory and
  honor.   Psalm 8:3–5

He determines the number of the
  stars
and calls them each by name.
Great is our LORD and mighty in
  power;
his understanding has no limit.
                    Psalm 147:4–5

The date I gazed at the night sky:

Where?

The impact it had on my understanding of God:

What I will remember between here and heaven:

40 *Pray the rosary*

How? The rosary is a series of eighty prayers said in a particular order, often aloud, interspersed with meditation on Jesus' life. The best way to count how many prayers have been said is to move your fingers along a string of beads that has been developed over centuries for that purpose. The beads are in a circle, with gaps between them, and the circle has an attachment at the end of which is a cross.

Hold the cross and say the Apostles' Creed (a statement of what Christians believe). On the first large bead pray the Lord's Prayer. On the next three small beads, pray three Hail Marys (a prayer blessing the Virgin Mary and Jesus). At this point you will have worked up the attachment and will be on the circle. At the join, pray the Gloria (words of praise giving glory to God). Now take time to meditate on one of five events in Jesus' life (called mysteries). Over recent years the convention has emerged of considering his birth on Mondays and Saturdays, his ministry on Thursdays, his death on Tuesdays and Fridays, and the resurrection on Wednesdays and Sundays. During or after your meditation, pray the Lord's Prayer again as you hold the next large bead. On the following ten small beads, pray Hail Marys. On a gap between beads, hold the chain and pray the Gloria. That is the end of the first sequence (called a decade). Repeat the sequence four times to work your way round the whole set of rosary beads.

The words of all these prayers and mysteries can be found by following the links at www.catholic.org.

What Should I Expect? One of the reasons people

find the rosary helpful is that it brings together discipline (praising God in a set way) and liberty (letting your mind wander imaginatively through events in Jesus' life). To begin with, the process is unfamiliar and the prayers seem repetitive. However, in time it becomes possible to say the prayers from memory while your mind is set free to think about the five "mysteries" that are set for the day.

Think of it like driving a car. At first the mechanics of driving occupy your entire attention, but in time they become so instinctive that you are free to think about the view and the conversation instead of what your feet and hands are doing.

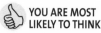

DON'T If you are not used to it, don't get overanxious about mentioning Mary in your prayers. Like other characters in the Bible, there is much in her life to emulate. Sense her example helping you to worship her son Jesus, and use the words "Hail Mary" in the same way that Gabriel did when he first said them to her (Luke 1:26–38).

YOU ARE MOST LIKELY TO THINK

The discipline of touching the beads has stopped my mind from wandering.

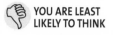

YOU ARE LEAST LIKELY TO THINK

I don't know what to say when I pray.

To Help You Reflect

I meditate on all your works
and consider what your hands have done.
I spread out my hands to you;
my soul thirsts for you like a parched land.
Answer me quickly, O LORD.

Psalm 143:5–7

Pray in the Spirit on all occasions with all kinds of prayers and requests. With this in mind, be alert and always keep on praying for all the saints.

Ephesians 6:18

The date I prayed the rosary:

A description of the beads I used:

Adjectives that describe the experience:

What I will remember between here and heaven:

41 *Keep a spiritual journal*

How? Invest in a book that is colorful and beautifully bound, so that it will give this a sense of importance and will be a pleasure to return to regularly. Either day by day or week by week, write a specialized diary. This is not just to keep a record of what has happened (although a brief summary of that will help you recall particular stages of your life when you revisit the book in years to come), but your personal response to spiritual matters.

Begin by writing the date. Imagine that Jesus is waiting outside the room, and that as soon as you have left he will come in and secretly read what you have written. What would you like to say to him?

Write quickly to record thoughts you have had about God and your place in the world. Document your feelings, doubts, and discoveries. Particularly mention the impact that relationships, events and new ideas have on you. Note what and for whom you are praying. Include Bible verses that register as significant, memories that resurface, and phrases from sermons, songs, books or television. As questions occur to you about your future, write them down as if you are having a conversation with yourself. Rebuke God when you need to. Paste in photographs or newspaper clippings if they make an impact on your emotions.

What Should I Expect? Some benefits of keeping

a spiritual journal are immediate and some only emerge over a period of time. When you begin to write, you will discover that you know truths that you did not realize you knew. You will come to the end of each day or week with an enhanced sense of achievement, because expressing your inner life on paper will make small ideas seem significant. Even if you have to record negative thoughts, unburdening yourself of them allows God's compassion to begin healing them.

Coming back to entries after a year or more allows you to track the paths down which God has led you and will reveal the progress you have made. Looking back at past hurts or crises and considering what they have subsequently allowed God to achieve in your life increases your confidence in trusting him for the future.

DON'T

Don't exaggerate or write in the hope of impressing someone. Be honest with yourself and God, and show no one else.

 **YOU ARE MOST LIKELY TO THINK**

I am learning what it means to live a worthwhile life. There is much that God needs to forgive, but over the course of time he is slowly preparing me for heaven.

YOU ARE LEAST LIKELY TO THINK

If my preparation for heaven is this slow I'll be dead before I get there.

To Help You Reflect

My son, do not forget my teaching, but keep my commands in your heart, for they will prolong your life many years and bring you prosperity. Let love and faithfulness never leave you; bind them around your neck, write them on the tablet of your heart. Then you will win favor and a good name in the sight of God and man.

Proverbs 3:1–4

Remember those earlier days after you had received the light, when you stood your ground in a great contest in the face of suffering . . . because you knew that you yourselves had better and lasting possessions. So do not throw away your confidence; it will be richly rewarded. You need to persevere.　Hebrews 10:32–36

The date I began to keep a spiritual journal:

What I intend to record in it:

The frequency with which I have decided to write:

What I will remember between here and heaven:

4 2 *Learn about jazz*

How? There is plenty of debate about the meaning of the word "jazz," but one fact is not up for speculation: jazz is a unique, American art form.

The beginning of jazz can be traced back to the early twentieth century in New Orleans, but its roots go far back into history. The traditions of both African and European music synthesized in the African American communities of the southern United States. Jazz was often played during a funeral procession, transporting the mourners to the cemetery with mournful tones that acknowledged the grief of those who had lost a loved one. After the funeral, as the people left the cemetery, the music turned to jubilation, a celebration of resurrection and new life.

Someone said, "Jazz is what feelings sound like." Jazz is something you have to experience. Reading about its history and origin is important, but to know jazz you have to listen to and feel the music.

Take a music appreciation class at a college. Go to venues where you can hear live jazz. Invite a friend to a jazz club. Hang around afterward, if you can. Ask the musicians questions. Just as you love to talk about what is of deepest importance to you, a professional musician is happy to share his or her love for jazz with a "newbie."

What Should I Expect? People have different tastes
in music. Some music grabs us the first time we hear it, and some music grows on us over time. Whether or not you have ever listened to much jazz, once you've learned its origins and history and listened to it with an informed ear, you will come away with a new appreciation for this American tradition.

DON'T

Don't stop once you've learned about jazz. Research other forms of music, especially music that varies from your usual taste.

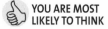 **YOU ARE MOST LIKELY TO THINK**

Wow! My spirit moves with the music.

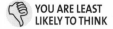 **YOU ARE LEAST LIKELY TO THINK**

I don't get it.

WHO SAYS?

Jazz does not belong to one race or culture, but is a gift that America has given the world.

Ahmad Alaadeen, jazz saxophonist and educator

To Help You Reflect

God has ascended amid shouts of joy, the LORD amid the sounding of trumpets.
Sing praises to God, sing praises.

Psalm 47:5–6

The date I attended a live jazz concert:

Three words that describe the experience:

How my understanding of jazz has changed:

What I will remember between here and heaven:

43 *Plant a tree*

How? Buy a sapling at a garden center or online. Choose a location at least 30 feet from buildings, and a tree that is appropriate to the space (perhaps a beech in a large garden or a wild cherry in a smaller one). Soak the roots of the tree. Dig a hole deep enough for the junction between the root and the stem to be at ground level when it is filled in. One person should hold the tree, shaking it gently so that the soil trickles through and around the roots as another person spades it in. Tread the soil firmly around the roots and water it well.

If a suitable space is not available, several schemes allow trees to be planted on your behalf in the developing world.

Check out the Arbor Day Foundation at www.arborday.org for information about planting and growing trees.

What Should I Expect?
Planting a tree is a determined act of faith that there will be a future for life on this planet after your own death, and for as long as God chooses to sustain his plan for humankind. It is a matter of simple generosity.

It is generous because it reverses the disastrous extent of carbon emissions, with their contribution to global warming, to which we add every time we use fuel. Trees recycle carbon dioxide into oxygen. Planting trees is an affirmation that the life of generations to come is more important than the lazy comfort of the generation that is presently alive. It may be done out of guilt at a wasteful lifestyle or out of a positive attempt to reverse an unsustainable trend—both speak of the repentance to which all the Bible's prophets call us.

It is also generous because others will enjoy the full benefit of the investment you are making, not you. Someone else's children will see the full-grown tree that you can only imagine. War, disease, or someone's whim could prevent it, but planting a tree despite the possibility of that happening is a statement that hope is a better way of life than cynicism. In that respect, it is an active prayer for the future of the place in which you have planted and the souls who will one day tread the paths you have trod.

DON'T

Don't plant fast-growing trees in a small suburban garden, because they grow so fast that they block the light and view of neighbors.

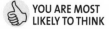 **YOU ARE MOST LIKELY TO THINK**

One day in the future someone still unborn will sit in the shade of this tree and be glad of what I have done.

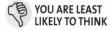 **YOU ARE LEAST LIKELY TO THINK**

I would like to have a bonfire.

To Help You Reflect

Be not afraid, O wild animals, for the open pastures are becoming green. The trees are bearing their fruit; the fig tree and the vine yield their riches. Be glad, O people of Zion, rejoice in the LORD your God, for he has given you the autumn rains in righteousness.

Joel 2:22–23

The angel showed me the river of the water of life, as clear as crystal, flowing from the throne of God. . . . On each side of the river stood the tree of life, bearing twelve crops of fruit, yielding its fruit every month. And the leaves of the tree are for the healing of the nations.

Revelation 22:1–2

The date I planted a tree:

Where and what type?

A message to people who will see the full-grown tree:

What I will remember between here and heaven:

44 Wash feet

How? Some churches have services of footwashing on the Thursday before Easter (Maundy Thursday). During the service the leaders of the church, following the example of Jesus, wash the feet of some or all of the congregation. This symbolic action requires the leaders to kneel humbly in front of people they lead with a bowl of warm water and a towel. A handful of water is poured over just one foot, which is then dried. In variations of this pattern, sometimes each member of the congregation washes the feet of a neighbor—usually men serving men and women serving women. It is almost always followed by Communion.

Telephone the offices of local churches as Easter approaches and ask whether they know of a service locally at which a foot washing will be held.

What Should I Expect?

In the time of Jesus foot washing was a courtesy to guests who arrived at your house having walked through dusty streets in open sandals. It was the slightly unpleasant task of a slave. The night before he died, Jesus put himself in the place of a slave by washing the feet of his embarrassed followers. His intention was to give a radically different model of leadership that is expressed through humility, rather than expecting deference.

The tradition of washing feet in Christian worship dates back to the second century. It is a reminder to congregations that leaders are there not to be served, but to serve. It is a humbling experience for the person who washes the feet, but it is equally moving for the people whose feet are washed, since it requires them to walk barefoot and vulnerable among friends and strangers.

Expect to feel challenged by God about your place in the community and whether you have been held back from giving others the help they need by pride or embarrassment. It is also a time to reflect that we sometimes feel unable to ask for help because that suggests weakness, and to be aware that although that is the way of the world, it has no place in Christian experience.

DON'T

Don't arrive with feet that actually do need washing. This should remind everyone of the need for humility, not hygiene.

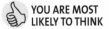 **YOU ARE MOST LIKELY TO THINK**

I am completely humbled by the sacrifice of Jesus.

 **YOU ARE LEAST LIKELY TO THINK**

A mark of how successful my life has been is never having to ask anyone for help.

WHO SAYS?

Lord of eternity dwells in humanity,
kneels in humility and washes our feet.
O what a mystery, meekness and majesty,
bow down and worship for this is your God.
Graham Kendrick, composer, from the hymn
"Meekness and majesty"

To Help You Reflect

Jesus knew that the Father had put all things under his power, and that he had come from God and was returning to God; so he got up from the meal, took off his outer clothing, and wrapped a towel around his waist. After that, he poured water into a basin and began to wash his disciples' feet, drying them with the towel that was wrapped around him.   John 13:3–5

[Jesus] turned toward the woman and said to Simon, "Do you see this woman? I came into your house. You did not give me any water for my feet, but she wet my feet with her tears and wiped them with her hair. You did not give me a kiss, but this woman, from the time I entered, has not stopped kissing my feet. You did not put oil on my head, but she has poured perfume on my feet. Therefore, I tell you, her many sins have been forgiven—for she loved much."   Luke 7:44–47

The date I took part in a footwashing service:

Where?

Name of the person whose feet I washed, or who washed mine:

What I will remember between here and heaven:

45 *Write a statement of faith*

How? Week after week, if we attend worship on a regular basis, we hear the word of God preached by a person who is trained to study the Scripture and use reliable resources to interpret this word to the congregation.

Thousands upon thousands of books have been written in an attempt to understand and explain the doctrines of faith.

What if someone asked you to sum up in one page what you believe? It would be a challenge, but one well worth taking, because we each should be able to articulate our beliefs in our own words.

Fold a sheet of paper in half horizontally, then in half again vertically. This gives you four squares in which to organize your thoughts. Write "God" in the first square, "Jesus" in the second, "Holy Spirit" in the third, and "Life" in the fourth. The first three categories are somewhat obvious; the fourth, "Life," is to express your beliefs about how the first three connect to all life, and to yours in particular.

Jot down the first words and thoughts that come to mind for each category. Don't feel as though you have to make comprehensive notes all at once. Let your notes sit awhile. Make notes "as the Spirit moves you."

Next, form your notes and thoughts into sentences. Limit yourself to no more than five sentences for each of the four themes. Setting limits helps you condense and articulate your beliefs in a succinct way.

Finish by writing a one-page summary of your beliefs. Can't stop at one page? Maybe you'll end up writing a book yourself someday!

What Should I Expect?

You may be surprised at how well you can summarize your faith beliefs, or you may find it frustrating trying to put your beliefs into words. If the latter is the case, this may signal that an aspect of your faith needs a little more thought and exploration. That's not a bad thing. Faith should be living and real, and learning to express your changing understanding of faith and life ought to be a lifelong journey.

Have fun! Nobody is going to grade you. You're doing this for yourself. This is between you and God.

DON'T

Don't give up. Your statement of faith may never be quite finished. Feel free to edit whenever you wish.

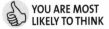 **YOU ARE MOST LIKELY TO THINK**

This isn't easy—but it sure is interesting!

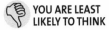 **YOU ARE LEAST LIKELY TO THINK**

Now that I've written down what I believe, I don't have to think about it anymore.

WHO SAYS?

If you must tell me your opinions, tell me what you believe in. I have plenty of doubts of my own.
—Johann Goethe

To Help You Reflect

Always be prepared to give an answer to everyone who asks you to give the reason for the hope that you have. But do this with gentleness and respect.
1 Peter 3:15

Ever since I heard about your faith in the Lord Jesus and your love for all the saints, I have not stopped giving thanks for you, remembering you in my prayers. I keep asking that the God of our Lord Jesus Christ, the glorious Father, may give you the Spirit of wisdom and revelation, so that you may know him better. I pray also that the eyes of your heart may be enlightened in order that you may know the hope to which he has called you, the riches of his glorious inheritance in the saints, and his incomparably great power for us who believe. That power is like the working of his mighty strength.
Ephesians 1:15–19

The date I first took notes, and the date I finished writing my statement of faith:

What surprised me most about my beliefs:

My favorite sentence:

What I will remember between here and heaven:

46 *Help people register to vote*

How? Voting is one of our rights and responsibilities as free citizens.

You need to be a U.S. citizen, and 18 years of age by Election Day, in order to vote. Contact your state or county board of elections to discover any other requirements. Two forms of identification are required to register.

Registering to vote is easier than ever. The League of Women Voters (www.lwv.org) provides information such as how to find your polling place, deadlines for registration, and state amendments. With online resources, you may not even have to leave home.

Know the stance of the candidates and find out the issues that are on your ballot. Newspapers often print helpful guides in the months and weeks prior to an election. Read, study, keep an open mind, and talk to people who both agree with and oppose your viewpoints. Clarify your reasons for supporting a particular candidate. If you are encouraging others to register to vote, it is important for you to state why voting is important to you and to your community.

Ask your friends if they are registered to vote. Offer to help those who aren't by walking them through the process online, or go with them to register in person.

When Election Day rolls around, offer to drive a group to the polls—make it an event! Vote together, go out to lunch, and watch the election returns on the evening news.

You should know registration deadlines, how to submit an absentee ballot, early voting options, ID requirements, and how to watch political debates with a critical eye.

What Should I Expect? You will learn a lot about the voting process and about yourself. As you study the issues and sort through your own beliefs, you may discover biases you never realized you had. Be open to changing your mind. You may also find that you are motivated to speak out about an issue. Even if you are reserved or shy by nature, expect to surprise yourself, as well as others, with the strength of your ability to articulate your understanding of the issues.

DON'T Don't give up too soon. If most of your family and friends are already registered to vote, check with a local college campus and see if you can help register first-time voters.

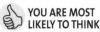

YOU ARE MOST LIKELY TO THINK

I am glad to live in a country where we have the freedom to vote.

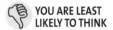

YOU ARE LEAST LIKELY TO THINK

This was a worthless exercise.

WHO SAYS?

People often say that, in a democracy, decisions are made by a majority of the people. Of course, that is not true. Decisions are made by a majority of those who make themselves heard and who vote—a very different thing.

Walter H. Judd, physician, missionary, member of Congress, 1957 delegate to the United Nations

To Help You Reflect

" ... for the authorities are God's servants, who give their full time to governing."

Romans 13:6b

Therefore I glory in Christ Jesus in my service to God.

Romans 15:17

The date I helped someone register to vote:

Where we went to register:

The result of the election:

What I will remember between here and heaven:

47 *Take a new route to work*

How? Get off the bus one stop early and walk the rest of the distance. Or one stop late. Travel in the front car of a train instead of the back one. Jog instead of walking. Or turn left where you usually turn right and take a long cut. Share a car journey. Climb six flights of stairs instead of taking the elevator. Or use the ramp for wheelchair users instead of the stairs.

If you work in your own home, create an equivalent variation on your routine. Eat breakfast before you shower, or vice versa. Make yourself up to look stunning even though the only person who will see it is the baby. Get dressed listening to a different radio station. Or in silence!

What Should I Expect?
Be acutely aware of what you are doing, what you observe, and how you feel. For some, it will be a positive experience. They will notice details they had not seen before (for example, a house where the trash can is kept in a more logical place, a plant that is in flower at an unexpected time). They will discover shops they did not know were there, or be intrigued to perceive how the area seems different to someone pushing a stroller, riding a bicycle, or partially sighted. Others will find themselves irritated by the disruption to their routine, feeling that their time has been wasted, and that the new thoughts they have had are too insubstantial to have been worth the effort. Either will interrupt the usual patterns of your brain, and stimulate it to view other things in innovative ways.

We have a God who lives in a constant present, endlessly thinking new thoughts, and constantly reinventing the way the world is sustained in order to bring good out of confusion and love out of coincidence. Every new route for you becomes a new opportunity for God. With your eyes open to what God has to show you, your head will become open to what God might teach you, and your heart to the desire to align yourself with God's plan for the world.

DON'T Don't stop there! Eat lunch in a new place or at a different time, use the toilet on a different level, drink water instead of coffee, speak to a different colleague, rearrange your desk, change your computer screensaver, give customers their change with your left hand instead of your right, subtly change your form of words when you answer the telephone so that you sound more cheerful.

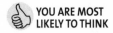

YOU ARE MOST LIKELY TO THINK

I never noticed that before!

YOU ARE LEAST LIKELY TO THINK

Today I am least likely to think!

To Help You Reflect

[The LORD declares:]
"I will lead the blind by ways they have not
known,
along unfamiliar paths I will guide them;
I will turn the darkness into light before them
and make the rough places smooth.
These are the things I will do;
I will not forsake them."

Isaiah 42:16

The date I took a new route to work:

What was different?

Things I noticed that I would not otherwise have seen:

What I will remember between here and heaven:

48 Walk the stations of the cross

How? Pilgrims visiting Jerusalem have, since the earliest days of Christianity, traced the route along which Jesus staggered carrying his cross to the execution site. It is known as the Via Dolorosa ("the grief-stricken way"). Walking the route was popularized during the fourteenth century by the Franciscan monks who were given custody of the sites associated with Jesus' life. Franciscans still lead a pilgrimage through the Jerusalem streets every Friday, starting at St. Stephen's Gate at 3 p.m. and stopping to pray at the presumed locations of particular events.

As pilgrims returned, thrilled by what they had seen in Jerusalem, churches responded by bringing Jerusalem to those who could not travel. They commissioned paintings and sculptures, placed at intervals either indoors or outdoors, to tell the story of Jesus' journey to Calvary, and encouraged people to walk along the sequence meditating on his suffering. By the eighteenth century the number was fixed at fourteen—eight events recorded in the Gospels and six from Christian legends. In recent years Pope John Paul II devised a new sequence using biblical events only, and a fifteenth is often added to mark Jesus' resurrection.

Today almost all Roman Catholic places of worship and a few Protestant churches have artwork of some kind to allow people to walk the stations of the cross. There is no set form of words to pray, although many churches provide extracts from Scripture to aid meditation, and there are occasions (Good Friday, for instance) when services are held in which a whole congregation walks together. The internet also has sequences of stations of the cross, and www.catholic.org is a portal to the best.

What Should I Expect? Although the Internet sites are beautiful and moving, the true value of doing this is as much the walk as the stations. As Jesus is seen to move along the grief-stricken way, so you are moving with him. Realize that you are walking the way of Christ to the very end, just as he will walk with you through life no matter how difficult or lonely that journey becomes.

DON'T

Don't finish your
meditation with Jesus
dead. Rejoice about
the fundamental
truth of the Christian
faith—that he lives.

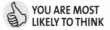 **YOU ARE MOST
LIKELY TO THINK**

All this for me!

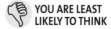 **YOU ARE LEAST
LIKELY TO THINK**

It was not worth doing
because it isn't historically
accurate.

WHO SAYS?

We adore you, O Christ, and we bless you, because by your holy cross,
you have redeemed the world.

*Francis of Assisi, founder of the Franciscan order, 1182–1226,
words that are used by tradition at every station*

To Help You Reflect

Christ suffered for you, leaving you an example, that you should follow in
his steps. "He committed no sin, and no deceit was found in his mouth."
When they hurled their insults at him, he did not retaliate; when he
suffered, he made no threats. . . . By his wounds you have been healed.

1 Peter 2:21–24

Is it nothing to you, all you who pass by? Look around and see. Is any
suffering like my suffering that was inflicted on me?

Lamentations 1:12

The date I walked the stations of the cross:

Where, and what was the style of the images?

The station that had the most meaning to me:

What I will remember between here and heaven:

49 *Contribute to Wikipedia*

How? Wikipedia is a vast encyclopedia on the Internet. Uniquely, it is free and accessible to anyone. It is written entirely by volunteers, and anyone in the world can contribute from their own expertise. It has not only an encyclopedia, but also the texts of history's most important books, speeches, and quotations. In the few years since it was founded in 2001, it has become one of the most most visited Web sites. It can be found at www.wikipedia.org.

Next to each of the three million articles is a tab to click if you wish to add information or correct something inaccurate. It is also possible to post an article about a new subject, but this requires you to register. Full instructions appear in the Wikipedia FAQs. An army of volunteers collaborates to develop it and guard against its abuse.

Before a full article is written, a brief paragraph (called a "stub") is posted, with an invitation to anyone with expertise or the ability to research the subject to expand it. Tens of thousands of these are waiting for attention. Browse them, find one about which you have information to add, edit it, and post it. If you do not know where to start, there are nearly 1,000 stubs related to Christianity alone. To find them, click on "Categories" in the middle of the main page, then on "Christianity" in the Religions section, and finally on "Christianity stubs" which is listed under S in the alphabetical list.

What Should I Expect? Wikipedia has critics who

point out that it is open to vandalism and each article is only as reliable as its last editor. While this is true, it is remarkable how little abuse happens. The desire to do good is genuinely defeating the desire to do harm.

The shared ideology of the Wikipedia community, that education should be freely available to every human being, is one of the few surviving remnants of the idealism of the Internet's founding fathers, before it was overwhelmed by pornography and spam. It also echoes the idealism of the first Christians in Jerusalem who sold their property and pooled their resources for the good of them all (although that too was vulnerable to trust being destroyed by a couple of selfish people).

DON'T

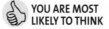 **YOU ARE MOST LIKELY TO THINK**

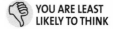 **YOU ARE LEAST LIKELY TO THINK**

Don't bluff, because you will be found out. If you do so maliciously, you will be blocked.

All the knowledge in God's world should be available to all the people of God's world.

It's not what you know; it's who you know.

WHO SAYS?

I'm doing this for the child in Africa who is going to use free textbooks and reference works produced by our community and find a solution to the crushing poverty that surrounds him.... And I'm doing this for my own daughter, whom I hope will grow up in a world where culture is free, not proprietary, and where control of knowledge is in the hands of people everywhere [without needing to ask] permission from anyone.

Jimmy Wales, founder of Wikipedia

To Help You Reflect

Wisdom is a shelter as money is a shelter, but the advantage of knowledge is this: that wisdom preserves the life of its possessor. Consider what God has done!

Ecclesiastes 7:12–13

Paul, a servant of God and an apostle of Jesus Christ for the faith of God's elect and the knowledge of the truth that leads to godliness—a faith and knowledge resting on the hope of eternal life.

Titus 1:1–2

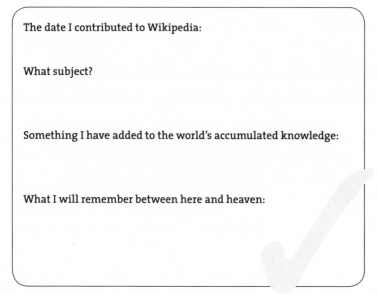

The date I contributed to Wikipedia:

What subject?

Something I have added to the world's accumulated knowledge:

What I will remember between here and heaven:

50 Find out about Islam

How? The Islamic Information Center helps people go beyond a cursory knowledge. Visit www.islamicinformationcenter.org and check the basic information about Islam, as well as current news events. *Islam, a Very Short Introduction* (Malise Ruthven, Oxford Paperbacks) requires concentration, but is rewarding. The Qur'an (Koran) is a much more complex book than the Bible and without a commentary you will be tempted to give up. Begin with *The Essential Koran: The Heart of Islam—A Selection of Introductory Readings* (Thomas Cleary, HarperOne).

Mosques vary between those which are geared up to welcome and inform non-Muslim guests, and those that regard visitors with polite caution.

According to Islam, there is only one God, who is our creator, sustainer, guide, and judge. It is the task of all humans to make the world a better place, and they do that by going beyond their natural inclination to selfishness. A series of prophets have revealed this to humankind through the ages. Muslims recognize Jesus as one of the most important (although they do not worship him as God), but the last and greatest is Muhammad, who is profoundly revered.

Five essential duties of all Muslims ("Pillars of Faith") are to proclaim that: "There is no God but Allah, and Muhammad is his prophet," to face Mecca and pray five times daily, to be generous to the poor, to fast from dawn until sunset throughout the month of Ramadan (mid-Autumn in the United States), and to make a pilgrimage to Mecca (Muhammad's birthplace).

What Should I Expect?

Expect to discover that the values at the heart of Islam are loving, charitable, and godly. About one billion people worldwide follow the teachings of Muhammad, who lived in the Middle East from 570 until 633. They are preserved in the Qur'an, written (and only valid) in Arabic following revelations to Muhammad from God, known by the name Allah.

DON'T Don't try to persuade yourself that Islam and Christianity are identical in all but name, but do recognize that Muslims are praying to the same God that Abraham and Jesus prayed to, and should have friendship, understanding, and respect.

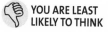

YOU ARE MOST LIKELY TO THINK

All Christians ought to learn these things in order to diminish fear and promote peace.

YOU ARE LEAST LIKELY TO THINK

I am full of hate.

WHO SAYS?

Jesus came with manifest proofs. He said, "Now I have come to you with wisdom. I will resolve for you some of the things about which you differ. Therefore, worship Allah, and obey my commands. This is the right way."

Holy Qur'an 43:62–63

To Help You Reflect

"The God who made the world and everything in it is the Lord of heaven and earth and does not live in temples built by hands. And he is not served by human hands, as if he needed anything, because he himself gives all men life and breath and everything else. From one man he made every nation of men, that they should inhabit the whole earth. . . . God did this so that men would seek him and perhaps reach out for him and find him, though he is not far from each one of us.

Acts 17:24–27

The LORD had said to Abram . . . "I will make you into a great nation and I will bless you; I will make your name great, and you will be a blessing."

Genesis 12:1–2

The date I found out about Islam:

How?

Something I learned that changed me:

What I will remember between here and heaven:

51 *Forgive a wrong*

How? This requires an act of will, rather than making an emotional decision. It is not like a contract between you and the person who has wronged you which requires him or her to do something in exchange. In fact, the other person doesn't even need to know that they have been forgiven. You need simply to decide that you are no longer going to let the wrong that has been done to you have a hold over you. You don't need to have the last word in an argument. You don't need to have got what you deserved (in fact, you probably haven't). You just need to let go.

The question of whether you tell the other person they are forgiven needs to be taken carefully. It may reopen aggravation and create yet another sin that needs to be forgiven. Alternatively, it may re-establish a relationship that will bring you both happiness. Or it may be that you can no longer contact the person anyway. Make a choice, and decide in advance not to let the consequences spoil the joy of having released yourself from the burden.

What Should I Expect?

You are not doing this for the benefit of the person who has wronged you. You are doing it to improve your own life. Of course, the side effect may be that the other person's situation improves too. It is possible that some of the ordinary joys of friendship may open up again for them. But the main point of forgiving a wrong is that you can be released from the power it has over you. After forgiving someone, you are no longer a victim. You have done something about the wrong that only you could do, and the person who inflicted it has no power to stop you. A burden will lift. Back in control of the situation you will discover that what the Bible says about the kingdom of God is true—in weakness there is a great strength.

You are treading a route that Jesus took when, with his dying breath, he chose to forgive his murderers. God did not begin to work the resurrection when the women arrived on the Sunday; he began it when the wrongdoing was forgiven on the Friday.

DON'T

Don't attach
conditions, because if
you constantly have to
monitor whether the
conditions are being
fulfilled you will not
be free of the burden.

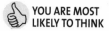 **YOU ARE MOST
LIKELY TO THINK**

I have got nothing to lose.
If it doesn't work, I can
always go back to the hate
and tension again. But I
just don't want to.

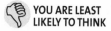 **YOU ARE LEAST
LIKELY TO THINK**

Obviously there is nothing
about me that needs to be
forgiven.

To Help You Reflect

[Jesus said,] "Be merciful, just as your Father is
merciful. Do not judge, and you will not be judged.
Do not condemn, and you will not be condemned.
Forgive, and you will be forgiven. Give, and it will
be given to you. A good measure, pressed down,
shaken together and running over, will be poured
into your lap. For with the measure you use, it will
be measured to you."   Luke 6:36–38

Bear with each other and forgive whatever
grievances you may have against one another.
Forgive as the LORD forgave you. And over all these
virtues put on love, which binds them all together
in perfect unity. Let the peace of Christ rule in your
hearts, since as members of one body you were
called to peace.   Colossians 3:13–15

The date I forgave a wrong:

Draw a symbol that will remind only you who or what
was involved:

What difference has it made to the relationship?

What I will remember between here and heaven:

52 *Learn yoga*

How? Not everyone can run a marathon, parachute from an airplane, or leap tall buildings in a single bound. But nearly anyone of any age or physical condition can learn some of the simple moves of yoga.

The thought of yoga may conjure up images of people twisting their bodies into pretzels and bending in unimaginable ways. Take heart! Those types of poses are for the experts.

Yoga classes can be found at fitness centers, college campuses, park districts, and even libraries. Books and DVDs are available at bookstores and health stores and online. It's best if you learn the basics from a qualified instructor so that you learn the proper postural alignment and breathing techniques. These basics alone make yoga a practice you can continue throughout your lifetime.

There are various types of yoga, so when you sign up for a class, ask the instructor what the class will cover. Yoga refers to both physical and mental disciplines. You may shy away from yoga, thinking that it goes against your spiritual beliefs. Learning the fundamentals of yoga will not compromise your faith. In fact, the quest for peace of mind, spiritual centeredness, and healthy movement can be an asset in your daily spiritual exercises. Yoga can help you sleep better. It's great for anyone, but especially for those who struggle with tight muscles and painful joints.

As is true before beginning any new physical exercise, check with your physician to be sure yoga is safe for you. You may want to look for a "chair yoga" class, in which yoga techniques are taught sitting on or using the support of a chair. Chair yoga is great not only for people who need the extra support, but also for anyone who travels or sits in an office for a good part of the day. Some of the stretches can be done so subtly, your coworkers won't even know. Better yet, share your knowledge! You might get your office to incorporate a little healthy chair yoga into the company lunchtime.

What Should I Expect?
You don't have to sweat to exercise your body. Yoga will give you energy, strength, an overall healthier outlook, and more restful sleep. After a session of yoga, you will be relaxed but energized. Yoga may help your heart rate and blood pressure.

DON'T

Don't push yourself
to the point of pain. If
your muscles or joints
begin to hurt, stop. "No
pain, no gain" is not
the motto of yoga.

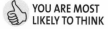 **YOU ARE MOST
LIKELY TO THINK**

I feel better after just one
session!

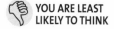 **YOU ARE LEAST
LIKELY TO THINK**

Yoga is for wimps.

WHO SAYS?

What happens when your soul
Begins to awake in this world
To our deep need to love
And serve the Friend?
Hafez, Persian mystic and poet

To Help You Reflect

Let everything that has breath praise
the LORD. Praise the LORD.

Psalm 150:6

Again Jesus said, "Peace be with
you! As the Father has sent me, I
am sending you." And with that he
breathed on them and said, "Receive
the Holy Spirit."

John 20:21–22

The place where I took my first yoga class:

My favorite pose:

How I felt after class:

What I will remember between here and heaven:

53 *Say grace*

How? Look at the food that is in front of you. Count the colors. Smell it and get ready to enjoy it, but hold back for a moment before taking a mouthful. Register that it is only because of the goodness of God and the work of many humans that the food is in front of you. Then tell God what you feel. If words do not come naturally, say: "Thank you, God, for this food and for all the good things you give us. Amen."

As saying grace becomes more natural, add variations by mentioning the name of the food or the people with whom you are sharing the occasion. If you are by yourself, take the opportunity to thank God for other good experiences of the day. If children are with you, make the words very simple, and consider holding hands around the table so that they have a sense of a special moment in God's company. Then dig in!

What Should I Expect? If you are going to be

thankful for your food you must be eating it in a context in which you are going to enjoy it. That is not going to happen if you are stuffing down a burger as you walk the street, if you are more interested in the television than the taste, or if you are in a family that is eating in three separate rooms. If those are the routines into which you have fallen, there is little evidence that you are grateful for the food you are eating, and God will not be fooled. Changing those routines will be five times more meaningful than saying a sentence before the first mouthful.

Be glad that God has put you in a world in which everything you need for survival exists. Then be amazed that God has chosen to do this by providing an inexhaustible variety of flavors, textures, and colors.

As it becomes habitual to pause before you eat and acknowledge that you would not be alive without God nourishing you, you will become more connected with the creator. You will also notice that you are making connections with the people through whose hands the plants or animals have passed on their way to your plate, some of whom thrive and profit as a result of it, and others who suffer injustice because of the nature of trade and find themselves in poverty, ill health, or despair. Let your prayer expand into a plea for justice and change.

DON'T

Don't try to be witty or clever. The point is not to entertain or impress the others around the table; it is to thank God.

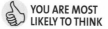 **YOU ARE MOST LIKELY TO THINK**

I am grateful for those who have made this meal possible.

 **YOU ARE LEAST LIKELY TO THINK**

This is just a meaningless ritual done by thoughtless people.

WHO SAYS?

You say grace before meals. All right, but I say grace before the concert and the opera, and grace before the play and pantomime, and grace before I open a book, and grace before sketching, swimming, fencing, boxing, walking, playing, dancing, and grace before I dip the pen in ink.

G.K. Chesterton, novelist, 1874–1936

To Help You Reflect

Praise the LORD, O my soul. . . .
He makes grass grow for the cattle,
and plants for man to cultivate—
bringing forth food from the earth:
wine that gladdens the heart of man,
oil to make his face shine,
and bread that sustains his heart.

Psalm 104:1, 14–15

Taking the five loaves and the two fish and looking up to heaven, [Jesus] gave thanks and broke the loaves. Then he gave them to his disciples to set before the people. He also divided the two fish among them all. They all ate and were satisfied.

Mark 6:41–42

The date I began to say grace regularly:

What did I eat that day?

How will I remind myself to do this without fail?

What I will remember between here and heaven:

54 *Investigate your Christian name*

How? Visit www.behindthename.com and type in your name. Having found its meaning, follow the links to discover its history, popularity over the past century, and anecdotes about people who have shared your name in life or literature. If it is possible, contact the people who gave you your name, or relatives who were alive at the time, and discover whether you were named after anyone, or the thinking that went into it. If you have changed your name, revisit the circumstances that led you to choosing it. When you have gathered all the information you can, spend some time thinking about your name, the way it has shaped your character, and whether it can reveal anything of God to you.

Do you like it? Does its meaning have any relation to events that have taken place in your life? Has the person for whom you were named had an influence on your life? Are there things about your life that have been held back by the name that you have been carrying with you? Does the fact that it is your Christian name have a spiritual significance for you?

What Should I Expect? Changes of name in the
Bible mark turning points. The first leader of the church had his name changed by Jesus from Simon ("listening") to Peter ("rock"). Saul changed to its Roman equivalent Paul ("small and unassuming," which he wasn't, but which expressed the humility of Jesus, his role model).

Some names in the Bible are given in the knowledge that they will be momentous. For example, Ahikim means "my brother lives again," and it is easy to picture the tragic circumstances in which he received the name, and the burden it is for someone to grow up with such expectations. Other names must simply have appealed to a mother and father. Deborah sweetly means "bee," and one can imagine the cooing and cuddling that was offered to a little Jewish girl with such a name. It may be that understanding where your name came from explains expectations that people have placed on you, opening you to rejoice in God's presence at the love that welcomed you into the world, or to seek God's healing for a burden that you have had to bear.

DON'T

Don't use discoveries about your name to predict the years ahead in a superstitious way. This exercise is about reflecting on how your past has led you to this moment and does not have any power to ruin your future.

 **YOU ARE MOST LIKELY TO THINK**

This is my Christian name, the name by which God knows me, and it is this name I will hear calling me when I am lovingly welcomed into God's presence.

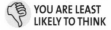 **YOU ARE LEAST LIKELY TO THINK**

I wish they had calld me Abishag. (It means "My father got up to no good," 1 Kings 1:3)

WHO SAYS?

A signature always reveals a person's character. Sometimes it even reveals his name.
Evan Esar, North American writer, 1899–1995

To Help You Reflect

But now, this is what the LORD says . . .
"Fear not, for I have redeemed you;
I have summoned you by name; you are mine."
Isaiah 43:1

[God says,] "Can a mother forget the baby at her breast
and have no compassion on the child she has borne?
Though she may forget, I will not forget you!
See, I have engraved you on the palms of my hands."
Isaiah 49:15–16

The day I thought about the origin of my Christian name:

This is what it means and this is how I come to have the name:

How does my life compare with the meaning of my name?

What I will remember between here and heaven:

55 *Learn the globe*

How? The geography you learned growing up has probably changed. The globe that sat in your grandfather's study is a lovely keepsake, but don't use it when you're helping your kids with their homework.

Compare a map from 1945 to one from 1965 and you'll find changes in our own nation, with the last two states admitted into the union (Alaska and Hawaii, both in 1959). Other countries have undergone changes in boundaries, names, and identities. Check the history of the former Socialist Federal Republic of Yugoslavia, the former Union of Soviet Socialist Republics, and the continent of Africa, and see how many former and current countries you can name.

In the years from 1990 to 2005, more than thirty new nations were created. How are those of us who are already geographically challenged supposed to keep track of such vast changes?

Your library will have current and past atlases. Find several with publication dates ten years apart (for instance, 1980, 1990, and 2000) and open them up to the same area of the world. Make notes about what you find (or what you don't find!). Read the histories of countries that have undergone the most change, and find out why these changes occurred. Why is the world's geography in such flux?

Many online resources provide interactive maps, and satellite views. Look at earth.google.com, maps.live.com, and maps.nationalgeographic.com/maps.

What Should I Expect? Keep in mind that the

changes in the world's borders are often the result of upheaval and war. The world is more than rivers and oceans and mountains and deserts indicated on a map. Studying the changes will make you more aware of the people living in parts of the world you may never even have heard about.

The evening news will make more sense, too. You will be more likely to pay attention to news stories from far-flung places. Your worldview will be broadened in far more ways than one.

DON'T

Don't think the world will ever be static. It won't!

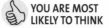 **YOU ARE MOST LIKELY TO THINK**

Geography is more than shading a map with colored pencils.

 **YOU ARE LEAST LIKELY TO THINK**

It doesn't matter what is happening on the other side of the world.

WHO SAYS?

Education is the most powerful weapon which you can use to change the world.
Nelson Mandela, South African political leader

To Help You Reflect

The earth is the Lord's, and everything in it, the world, and all who live in it.

Psalm 24:1

A country I never heard of before:

Something about the world I never knew:

My plan to keep updated on the changing world:

What I will remember between here and heaven:

56 *Get acquainted with community help services*

How? We never know when an emergency might strike in our own lives or in the lives of family, friends, and neighbors. Knowing in advance what community resources are available can save valuable time when you need it.

Keep a phone list of the police station, ambulance service, hospitals, and funeral homes in a place where it can be located easily in an emergency. Check the numbers several times a year to be sure they are up to date. You can always call 911 in an immediate crisis.

The U.S. Department of Health and Human Services' Substance and Mental Health Services Administration keeps a list of toll-free phone numbers for hotlines in the United States. Visit www.mentalhealth.samhsa.gov/hotlines for a current list plus additional information.

Not everyone is qualified to counsel others through a time of crisis or grief. However, you may be able to help someone going through a situation similar to your own. The Lung Cancer Alliance (www.lungcanceralliance.org) provides opportunities to serve as a "Phone Buddy" and provide the support of a good listener or to volunteer with a hotline. Other support agencies offer similar options.

What Should I Expect?
We never know when a sudden crisis will strike. Even though there is no way to be fully prepared, it helps to have information readily available when you are not necessarily thinking straight.

It is our nature to want to help people who are suffering or grieving. There is so much we cannot do: we cannot solve the problems they have to face or make the pain go away. But we can provide information and be a source of strength and support. Learn to be a good listener: admit your limitations, but simply be present. When a person has suffered a deep loss or critical illness, the worst thing you can do is to pretend that nothing is happening or that nothing has changed. Call or stop by to talk, but don't push it. Respect a person's privacy. Keep in touch. A phone call six months after the funeral to let your friend know you haven't forgotten their loss means a great deal.

DON'T

Don't ever tell someone who has been bereaved what they ought to think or feel.

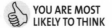 **YOU ARE MOST LIKELY TO THINK**

To be allowed to share someone's grief is to be invited into the part of their life that is most precious and spiritually alive.

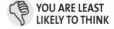 **YOU ARE LEAST LIKELY TO THINK**

Cheer up!

WHO SAYS?

Be not hasty to offer advice to those who are bowed down with a weight of trouble. There is a sacredness in grief which demands our reverence; the very habitation of a mourner must be approached with awe.

Charles Simeon, clergyman, 1759–1836

To Help You Reflect

[Jesus said,] "Blessed are those who mourn, for they will be comforted."

Matthew 5:4

Brothers, we do not want you to be ignorant about those who fall asleep, or to grieve like the rest of men, who have no hope. We believe that Jesus died and rose again and so we believe that God will bring with Jesus those who have fallen asleep in him.

1 Thessalonians 4:13–14

The date I helped someone in a crisis:

What were the circumstances?

Some of the emotions of which I was aware:

What I will remember between here and heaven:

57 *Listen to a choral masterpiece*

How? Find details of concerts in newspapers or from the brochures of concert halls. You can identify choral concerts because the name of the choir performing will be listed. Check the listings in your newspaper for churches, concert halls, and arenas where concerts take place. Use the Internet and search for "find choir concert" for events in your area.

Your library will have music you can borrow and enjoy at home or in the car. Soothing music is a good way to pass the time while you are on the road or as you are drifting off to sleep after a long day.

Readily enjoyable works include *Spem in alium* (by the sixteenth-century composer Thomas Tallis—an undulating sea of harmonies whose words mean, "I have never put my hope in anyone but you, God"), Messiah (by George Handel, an eighteenth-century oratorio about the significance of Jesus), and Mass in B minor (by Johann Sebastian Bach, a setting of the Latin words used in a Communion service). Contemporary masterpieces include Song for Athene (by John Tavener, interweaving words from a funeral service with others from Shakespeare's *Hamlet*, "Flights of angels sing thee to thy rest").

What Should I Expect? Most European choral masterpieces are settings of Christian texts. As the music proceeds, try to recognize the moods and make connections with experiences in the Christian life—mystery, sadness, yearning, and occasionally triumphant joy. If the piece is performed well you will glimpse these even without knowing the meaning of the words.

Listening to a choral masterpiece requires no previous knowledge. Simply let the music affect you—awakening feelings, activating memories, touching your heart. Concert "etiquette" (that is, applauding when the piece is finished, not between movements) can be learned by watching others.

If you are listening to live classical music for the first time, notice different speeds and instrument sounds, loudness and softness, and the way the voices of the choir blend together. As the musicians, doing something difficult with great skill, create a united sound, bring to mind God's desire to draw all humankind together in harmony with God.

DON'T

Don't sing along, even if you recognize the tune.

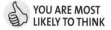 **YOU ARE MOST LIKELY TO THINK**

These voices, rising and falling in harmony, have set my mind on heaven.

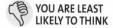 **YOU ARE LEAST LIKELY TO THINK**

Come back, Sex Pistols, all is forgiven!

WHO SAYS?

The aim and final end of all music should be none other than the glory of God and the refreshment of the soul.

Johann Sebastian Bach, composer, 1685–1750

To Help You Reflect

In a loud voice [the angels] sang: "Worthy is the Lamb, who was slain, to receive power and wealth and wisdom and strength and honor and glory and praise!" Then I heard every creature in heaven and on earth and under the earth and on the sea, and all that is in them, singing: "To him who sits on the throne and to the Lamb be praise and honor and glory and power, for ever and ever!"

Revelation 5:12–13

Sing joyfully to the LORD, you righteous;
it is fitting for the upright to praise him.
Praise the LORD with the harp;
make music to him on the ten-stringed lyre.
Sing to him a new song;
play skillfully, and shout for joy.

Psalm 33:1–3

The date I listened to a choral masterpiece:

The title, composer, and performers:

What aspect of God does the work celebrate?

What I will remember between here and heaven:

---

58 Sell your possessions at a flea market

How? A flea market doesn't sound like a very appealing place to shop, but you may find it a way to unload a lot of unneeded stuff.

A flea market tends to take place outdoors but may be held indoors. For a small fee, you can bring a load of items to sell (or trade): clothes, toys, jewelry—anything goes. What you thought of as junk can end up being another person's treasure.

Using your computer's Web browser, type in "flea market" to find a flea market in your vicinity. Some communities have flea markets on a regular basis that attract shoppers from miles away.

Even before you've found a location, you can start packing up the items you hope to sell. Set aside an area of your house or garage with boxes for gathering supplies. Go through your home closet by closet or room by room. Get rid of clothes you haven't worn in a year. Visualize the freedom from dusting knickknacks that don't have any sentimental value to you.

If you're not sure about getting rid of something, put it in a separate box, write the date on it, and set it aside. If you haven't had the urge to get that item after one year, you probably won't miss it once it's gone. Put the box with your "sell" items.

Talk to others about what you should charge for your items or attend a couple of flea markets before signing up, so you can get a feel for how the process works.

Don't replace your unneeded items with more of the same. If you donate your proceeds to charity, that may be incentive enough to unload, not load up.

What Should I Expect? When Jesus told his
followers to sell their possessions and give the money to the poor, he cannot have imagined flea markets. However, he did realize that the clutter distracts you from following him. His first followers sold anything they did not need (and much that they did) and with it created a fund that strengthened vulnerable people. This was so impressive to outsiders that they joined the church in large numbers.

Devise a plan to do good with your profits. Anticipate that someone will have their life improved in a way that is quite unexpected.

DON'T

Don't hoodwink a customer, since you are subject to trading standards law even if you only do this once in a lifetime, and must give a refund if you describe goods inaccurately.

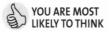 **YOU ARE MOST LIKELY TO THINK**

My life is better without this clutter, so I will do something worthwhile with the profit.

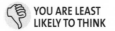 **YOU ARE LEAST LIKELY TO THINK**

I wish I hadn't parted with that lava lamp.

WHO SAYS?

I am still looking for the modern day equivalents of those Quakers who ran successful businesses, made money because they offered honest products and treated their people decently, worked hard, spent honestly, saved honestly, gave honest value for money, put more back than they took out, and told no lies.

Anita Roddick, founder of The Body Shop cosmetic retail chain

To Help You Reflect

All the believers were together and had everything in common. Selling their possessions and goods, they gave to anyone as he had need. Every day they continued to meet together in the temple courts. They broke bread in their homes and ate together with glad and sincere hearts, praising God and enjoying the favor of all the people. And the LORD added to their number daily those who were being saved.

Acts 2:44–47

The date I sold my possessions at a flea market:

My profit at the end of the day:

My best sales:

What I will remember between here and heaven:

59 *Have an alternative Christmas*

How? Many projects for vulnerable people need extra volunteers at Christmas because the usual lines of support close for the holiday. In particular, projects for homeless people offer shelter, food, and companionship during the coldest nights of the year. They require specialist volunteers, and those who can offer general help with serving meals and befriending guests.

You can find volunteer opportunities in your area by going to www.volunteermatch.org and typing in the name of your city and the type of service with which you are seeking to help, for instance, "homeless." Other nationwide agencies, such as Habitat for Humanity (www.habitat.org) and the Salvation Army (www .salvation army.org), need volunteers year-round, not just during the holidays. Perhaps you can make a New Year's resolution to get involved with helping others on a regular basis. Contact the organization requesting volunteers and find out whether you can match its needs with your availability. They will provide forms and guide you through the application process.

What Should I Expect? Christmas can be a time
of indulgence, so it is natural that Christians are eager to give it a practical meaning by serving vulnerable people. Because Mary and Joseph were essentially homeless when they arrived in Bethlehem, it is appropriate that thoughts turn particularly to those who are homeless. And because Christmas recognizes that God has been born among us, spending the holiday alongside those who need to experience his love and care is an obvious alternative to focusing on food and entertainment.

Some people volunteer their time in the service of others at Christmas expecting to feel richly fulfilled, but end up exhausted rather than elated. You ought to bear in mind, when you choose a project, that your objective is the pleasure that others will have. That would reflect Jesus' own actions, emptying himself of every aspect of his heavenly existence in order to be born in poverty, completely vulnerable, and without any kind of guarantee that the sacrifice would be acknowledged or welcomed by those he came to save.

DON'T

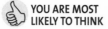 **YOU ARE MOST LIKELY TO THINK**

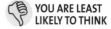 **YOU ARE LEAST LIKELY TO THINK**

Don't deprive someone whom you know of the time they genuinely need to share with you because of your determination to be generous to strangers.

If Jesus was on earth now, this is how he would have spent today.

Drat! I missed the annual Christmas special!

WHO SAYS?

Use your discernment and choose the course that takes you farthest away from the deadening activities of the stifling world, and brings you close to God. Direct your footsteps toward Bethlehem like the blessed Magi, your fellow companions, until you reach the appointed place of that blessed star.

Babai, leader of the church in Assyria, 551–628

To Help You Reflect

The grace of God that brings salvation has appeared to all men. It teaches us to say "No" to ungodliness and worldly passions, and to live self-controlled, upright and godly lives in this present age, while we wait for the blessed hope.

Titus 2:11–13

Your attitude should be the same as that of Christ Jesus: Who, being in very nature God, did not consider equality with God something to be grasped, but made himself nothing, taking the very nature of a servant, being made in human likeness.

Philippians 2:5–7

The date I spent Christmas in an alternative way:

What I did and where:

How did it improve someone else's life?

What I will remember between here and heaven:

60 *Analyze yourself with Myers-Briggs*

How? Two North American psychologists, Katharine Briggs and her daughter Isabel Myers, devised a test in 1940 that helps people understand why their personality leads them to prefer working, praying, and relating to others in a particular way. Influenced by Carl Jung's theories, the test involves ninety-three questions that ask you to choose between alternatives such as, "Are you more interested in starting projects or finishing projects?" The answers, once analyzed, position you on scales according to your preferences. These divide people into sixteen distinct personality types.

The test lends itself to exploring your spirituality, as well as your personality. Courses are widely available, and many retreat centers (listed at www.retreats.org) run them regularly or may be able to help you find one. *Knowing Me, Knowing God: Exploring Your Spirituality with Myers-Briggs*, by Malcolm Goldsmith (Abingdon, 1997), is a book that allows you to take the test by yourself. It can also be taken online at www .discoveryourpersonality.com/ MBTI.html, where the service includes a written report and a telephone consultation.

What Should I Expect? The scales show your

preference between Extrovert and Introvert (E/I—preferring to focus on the external world of objects and people, or the inner world of ideas and feelings); Sensing or Intuition (S/N—perceiving the world directly through the five senses, or processing the information through the unconscious to produce intuitive responses); Thinking or Feeling (T/F—making decisions in rational "true or false," or individualized "better or worse" ways); and Judging or Perceiving (J/P—preferring a step-by-step approach with rules that lead to a conclusion, or an approach that leaves options open and relies on subjective judgments). Together they create a four-letter personality type (for instance, ESTJ).

Knowing your personality helps you understand yourself, but it is also important for understanding others. What you once saw as inexplicably irritating attitudes emerge as strengths that can complement your own weaknesses in a team or congregation. It can lift guilt about not finding it easy to pray in a particular way and open possibilities for drawing closer to God.

DON'T

Don't assume that because you have a particular personality you cannot operate in any other way. Your type shows why you like certain things, not that you are incapable of doing others (just as left-handed people don't give up using their right hand). For instance, temperamentally Sensing people are capable of sitting through a sermon, although there are better ways for them to learn about God.

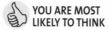 **YOU ARE MOST LIKELY TO THINK**

I now understand that people who disagree with me about how to worship, learn, and serve God are not wrong, just different.

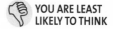 **YOU ARE LEAST LIKELY TO THINK**

Of course, the way I do it is better.

To Help You Reflect

There are different kinds of gifts, but the same Spirit. There are different kinds of service, but the same Lord. There are different kinds of working, but the same God works all of them in all men. Now to each one the manifestation of the Spirit is given for the common good.

1 Corinthians 12:4–7

He who gets wisdom loves his own soul; he who cherishes understanding prospers. . . . A man's wisdom gives him patience; it is to his glory to overlook an offense.

Proverbs 19:8, 11

The date I took a Myers-Briggs test:

My personality type:

Something I understood about myself for the first time:

What I will remember between here and heaven:

61 *Give to the world's poorest people*

How? Consider which of the many charities that fund work in the developing world best matches your ideas. A large organization that benefits many people, or a small one that funds a few specific projects? A Christian charity that includes prayer in its methodology, or a secular one that brings together generous people of all faiths and none? An organization that campaigns to change the root causes of poverty, or one that responds to emergencies with aid? Visit www.CharityNavigator.org to research a charity before you decide to donate time or money. This Web site provides helpful information that will enable you to choose a charity you can trust. Once you've chosen a charity, you can donate directly online or request information to be sent to you. Some charities even have programs through which you can make collections in your neighborhood, which helps save postage costs for the charity, allowing more money to go for its work.

What Should I Expect? From the very beginning

of God's dealings with his people, practical action for the poor has been singled out as the clearest evidence of a life lived as God intends. The Old Testament laws made provision for widows, orphans, and refugees unable to fend for themselves. It was not a handout, but a system that allowed poor people the dignity of working their own way out of poverty. Jesus, announcing the priorities of his mission, quoted a passage from Isaiah about bringing good news to the poor and relieving the plight of those who were suffering. And the letters of the New Testament, written during a time of famine, give explicit instructions to Christians who had more than enough to give money to those in need.

Each subsequent generation of Christians—the desert fathers, the Franciscans, the Victorian reformers, present-day campaigners—has made the pursuit of justice for those who have been made poor by the luxury of others central to the expression of their faith. So you should feel satisfied to be part of a centuries-old desire to reflect the compassion and justice that is in God's own nature.

DON'T

Don't make the arrangement through a person who stops you in the street. The agency organizing this will charge the charity anything up to the first year's worth of your donation. To maximize the percentage of your money that goes to the developing world, make direct contact with a charity.

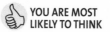 **YOU ARE MOST LIKELY TO THINK**

Giving money is just a start. Now I need to pressure politicians to change the circumstances that trap people in poverty.

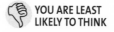 **YOU ARE LEAST LIKELY TO THINK**

What will they give me in return?

WHO SAYS?

The question to be asked is not, "What should we give to the poor?" but, "When will we stop taking from the poor?" The poor are not our problem; we are their problem.
Jim Wallis, founder of the Sojourners Community in Washington, D.C.

To Help You Reflect

The spirit of the Sovereign LORD is on me, because the LORD has anointed me to preach good news to the poor. He has sent me to bind up the brokenhearted, to proclaim freedom for the captives and release from darkness for the prisoners.   Isaiah 61:1

[Jesus said:] "Do not be afraid, little flock, for your Father has been pleased to give you the kingdom. Sell your possessions and give to the poor. Provide purses for yourselves that will not wear out, a treasure in heaven that will not be exhausted, where no thief comes near and no moth destroys. For where your treasure is, there your heart will be also."   Luke 12:32–34

The date I started a regular payment to the world's poorest people:

How much and to whom?

Which country or group of people inspired me to give?

What I will remember between here and heaven:

62 *Say the Jesus prayer*

How? The Jesus prayer dates back to the fifth century and is important in Orthodox traditions of Christianity. It involves repeating a short prayer to Jesus over and over again. The words often used are: "Lord Jesus Christ, Son of God, have mercy on me, a sinner" (words originally spoken by Bartimaeus to Jesus).

First, the words are spoken consciously and you concentrate on their meaning. Then the repetition allows you to enter a meditative state of prayer, in which you draw close to God in a way that is beyond words. Finally the words give way into a silence in which you and God are at rest in each other's company—what the Bible describes as "prayer without ceasing."

In Eastern Europe a rope of knots (chokti) is used to focus your mind. You hold the first knot between your fingers, say the prayer, then move to the next knot each time you repeat it. This is a less intrusive method than a clock for measuring how long you are at prayer.

What Should I Expect? The Jesus prayer is a way to allow adoration and repentance to descend from your mind to your heart, leaving you to gaze on God. There are no clever words said to impress other people. But it is far from meaningless, since it leads you into the same kind of humility that Jesus valued when he told a parable about a tax collector who was so conscious of his need of God that he was reduced to whispering these words repeatedly. You may find yourself drawn into an inner peace in which prayer has ceased to be something you do and has become something you are. In that state, God is able to make you deeply aware of the love God has for you, and of the absolute need you have for God as your savior. It is as if Jesus would gladly have given himself for you if you were the only needy human in the world.

DON'T

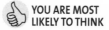 **YOU ARE MOST LIKELY TO THINK**

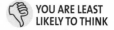 **YOU ARE LEAST LIKELY TO THINK**

Don't lose heart if you are distracted. Ease yourself back to the prayer knowing that, although your mind wandered away, Jesus did not.

I belong to my Lord and my Lord belongs to me. This is the most important thing in life.

I hope I have impressed other people by saying this.

WHO SAYS?

When I prayed with all my heart, everything around me seemed delightful and marvelous. The trees, the grass, the birds, the air, the light seemed to be telling me that they exist for the sake of humankind, that they witness to the love of God for humans, that all things pray to God and sing his praise.... I did not walk along as before, filled with care. The invocation of the name of Jesus gladdened my way. Everybody was kind to me. If anyone harmed me I had only to think, "How sweet is the Jesus Prayer," and the injury and the anger alike passed away.

The Way of a Pilgrim, an anonymous book of Orthodox spirituality, nineteenth century

To Help You Reflect

Through Jesus, therefore, let us continually offer to God a sacrifice of praise—the fruit of lips that confess his name.

Hebrews 13:15

The date I said the Jesus prayer:

For how long?

My feelings before, during, and after:

What I will remember between here and heaven:

63 *Clear out the cupboards*

How? Begin by hardening your heart. Then be pitiless! Get four boxes and label them: "Put away," "Give away," "Store away," and "Throw away." Start in the kitchen and work one cupboard at a time. Empty its contents completely and clean inside. Divide everything that was in it into one of the four boxes.

Pick up the items one at a time. If it is food that has passed its sell-by date, throw it away immediately. If you have never used it, make a snap decision about whether to throw it away or give it away, but resist all temptation to put it back. If you haven't used it in the last year, do the same. Particular ruthlessness is needed with equipment that was expensive (for example, the ten-year-old toasted sandwich maker in a greasy corner). The exceptions are things that are vital once a year, at Christmas, for instance, which could be stored in a place where they are not in the way. When you are left with items that you will certainly use, put them back in a logical order, with those you use daily easily accessible, and those you use less often on higher shelves.

Move on from the kitchen to other storage cupboards and drawers. Pay special attention to surfaces on which you tend to put things down haphazardly. Move on to tidy your CDs and DVDs (being unsentimental about things you no longer have the technology to play). If you have a garage or an attic, keep going!

What Should I Expect? Clearing away the clutter can also have a spiritual significance. As you find yourself letting go of things that have collected dust, you will find your attitude changing too. It is a kind of repentance, turning your back on what is unnecessary. Things that distract your attention from the way that God has laid out before you will disappear, people will become more important than objects, and you will become clearer about your priorities. You may even have a physical sensation of being cleansed, as though wrongdoing has been forgiven. When what is superfluous has gone from the house, and you look around to see what is left, you will find yourself looking at people you love, and you will sense God.

DON'T

Don't throw away anything that speaks of someone's love for you, even if that breaks all the rules you have decided on.

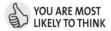 **YOU ARE MOST LIKELY TO THINK**

I'm going to keep it this way.

 **YOU ARE LEAST LIKELY TO THINK**

Oh how I wish I had kept that novelty jelly mold!

WHO SAYS?

If there is something you own that you can't give away, you don't own it—it owns you.

Albert Schweitzer, doctor and missionary to Africa, 1875–1965

To Help You Reflect

Whatever was to my profit I now consider loss for the sake of Christ. What is more, I consider everything a loss compared to the surpassing greatness of knowing Christ Jesus my LORD, for whose sake I have lost all things. I consider them rubbish, that I may gain Christ and be found in him.

Philippians 3:7–9

Do not store up for yourselves treasures on earth, where moth and rust destroy, and where thieves break in and steal. But store up for yourselves treasures in heaven, where moth and rust do not destroy, and where thieves do not break in and steal. For where your treasure is, there your heart will be also.

Matthew 6:19–21

The date I cleared out the cupboards:

I am glad to be rid of these:

I had forgotten I own these:

What I will remember between here and heaven:

64 *Ride a roller coaster*

How? The first roller coaster built in the United States emulated a runaway-train experience. The designers and builders of the Mauch Chunk Switchback Railway, in the mountains of Pennsylvania, could hardly have imagined the trend they began in 1873.

Roller coasters vary in building materials (steel and wood, to name a few), height, speed, and number of drops. From the Kinga Ka in Jackson, New Jersey, which boasts a 418-foot drop, to the 6,595-foot-long Millennium Force in Sandusky, Ohio, there's a roller coaster for every fan.

To find out more about roller coasters, and to locate the best roller coaster near you, check www.ultimaterollercoaster.com.

Tickets for most roller coasters can only be obtained as part of a day pass to a theme park containing many attractions. During school holidays, lines develop at the most popular rides, and it is wise to be at the park when it opens and go straight to the roller coaster that you want to ride. Careful attention is paid to safety in theme parks. Riders are very secure inside the car, but are responsible for ensuring that they do not lose hats, cash, or belongings.

What Should I Expect? Riding a roller coaster is basically a visceral experience, in which your body goes through extreme physical sensations. Those who enjoy roller coasters talk in particular about the excitement of surrendering to an experience that generates fear, but promises safety. The body has no control over what is happening to it and can feel weightless and heavy seconds apart. Those who hate roller coasters do so for the very same reasons.

To describe the experience as spiritual may be an exaggeration. However, a ride on a roller coaster makes you acutely aware of the body in which God has placed you, with its potential and limitations. Because your senses become first numb, and then intensely conscious, it is possible to become aware of both your connection to the earth on which all humans live, and also the difference between being alive and being clay. People who yelp with joy as they walk away from the ride may be praising God for their existence without even realizing it.

DON'T Don't risk your health if you know you have a medical condition that makes it unwise for your body to be put under strain. And don't get talked into doing something you are not confident about, because they won't stop the coaster for you once it has started.

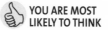 **YOU ARE MOST LIKELY TO THINK**

Aaaaaeea-eeoyee-ooo-iyaiyaiya-nthnthnth-errrrr-aaaaooa.

 **YOU ARE LEAST LIKELY TO THINK**

Now, let me analyze this intellectually!

To Help You Reflect

They mounted up to the heavens
and went down to the depths;
in their peril their courage melted away.

Psalm 107:26

I commend the enjoyment of life, because nothing is better for a man under the sun than to eat and drink and be glad. Then joy will accompany him in his work all the days of the life God has given him under the sun.

Ecclesiastes 8:15

The date I rode a roller coaster:

Where was it?

Adjectives that describe the experience:

What I will remember between here and heaven:

65 *Find your first home*

How? This may be easy (you may, for instance, still live in the house where you were born) or involve research and travel. If you know where you were born, visit by train, plane, or car. Walk around the area, trying to work out what remains from the date you were born, and what has been knocked down or redeveloped. Crouch, so that you can see the place from the perspective you had as a child. Introduce yourself to minimize the suspicion caused by someone loitering outside a house or taking photographs. If you do not know where you lived in your earliest days, begin by asking relatives. You may also be able to track down records through a Recorder of Deeds. Contact your local county clerk's office for details.

What Should I Expect?

Your experience will vary depending on whether you look back on your early years as joyful or miserable. Unless you left your birthplace at a very young age, the sights (and, more potently, the smells) will bring back recollections that would otherwise be buried. Looking at the setting to which your mother took you after your birth may help you understand the circumstances in which things happened when you were young, or may leave you with further questions that can only be answered by conversation with relatives.

As happy memories return, offer them to God, one by one, with thanksgiving. As unhappy memories arise, tell God about the healing that you need so that you will no longer be held back or trapped by the feelings they generate. Prepare to be disappointed by change or realization that your assumptions have been over-romantic—offer that to God as well. Whatever emotions arise, try to allow what you can see at your first home to help you understand more about why those who nurtured you in your infancy made the decisions they did.

DON'T Don't knock on the door of your first home and assume that the current occupant will spontaneously welcome a stranger in. If you wish to make contact, write in advance, prove your identity, treat the owner's caution with understanding, and be prepared to accept no for an answer.

YOU ARE MOST LIKELY TO THINK I have not traveled from this place to where I live today by a series of random accidents. God has journeyed with me and there has been a purpose to every turn of the route.

YOU ARE LEAST LIKELY TO THINK It's bigger than I expected.

WHO SAYS?

I remember, I remember,
The house where I was born,
The little window where the sun
Came peeping in at morn . . .
I remember, I remember,
The fir trees dark and high;
I used to think their slender tops
Were close against the sky:
It was a childish ignorance,
But now 'tis little joy
To know I'm farther off from heav'n
Than when I was a boy.

Thomas Hood, poet, 1799–1845

To Help You Reflect

You created my inmost being;
you knit me together in my
        mother's womb.
I praise you because I am fearfully
        and wonderfully made;
your works are wonderful,
        I know that full well.
My frame was not hidden from you
        when I was made in the secret
        place.

Psalm 139:13–15

The date I revisited my place of birth:

Where is it?

The difference between my expectations and the reality:

What I will remember between here and heaven:

66 *Buy nothing for a day*

How? Spend 24 hours living more simply, and without parting with cash, checks, or credit cards. This includes money spent on food, travel, entertainment, bills, and so on. For some regular purchases this will involve forgoing non-essentials (for instance, newspapers or snacks). For others, some planning will be involved. Work out how necessary travel can be paid for in advance, or walk. Use up food you have in the house instead of buying more. Pay bills in advance or the day after. Make presents for people instead of buying them. Think imaginatively about what could be borrowed or shared with friends. (There is no need to be pedantic about direct debits or subscriptions. This is a statement of intent, not a trial by ordeal.)

In the United States, "Buy Nothing Day" is supposed to be held on the Friday after Thanksgiving; ironically, one of the busiest shopping days of the year!

What Should I Expect? It is possible to treat a day without shopping as either a personal experiment or a public statement. Its purpose is not really to save money, but to increase your awareness of where your money goes. For example, to pay a bill the day before or the day after will not change the price, but will focus your mind more clearly on how much things cost, and whether they are really necessary.

Every time you register that you have had to change your routine in order to avoid spending money, bring to mind some of the issues involved in being a consumer. Twenty per cent of the world's population consumes 80 per cent of the resources God has placed on the earth, causing an unfair division of the world's wealth and a disproportionate level of environmental damage.

Lasting for a day without buying anything is more challenging than it appears. One person's stance will not, of course, have any impact at all on retailers, and the country will not grind to a halt. However, you may end the day feeling that you have more control over your life than usual. And it may lead you to make a decision to consume less, recycle more, and to pressure corporations to do their business in a cleaner and fairer way.

DON'T

Don't risk your health or happiness. Check the day before that you have first aid and that you are not going to offend friends.

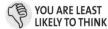 **YOU ARE MOST LIKELY TO THINK**

Can I do without it? Could I borrow one? Can I clean or repair it myself, rather than pay for it to be done? How will I dispose of it when I have finished with it? What are the environmental consequences of using it? Is there anything I already own that I could substitute?

YOU ARE LEAST LIKELY TO THINK

I can't afford to do that again.

To Help You Reflect

[Jesus said,] "Do not worry, saying, 'What shall we eat?' or 'What shall we drink?' or 'What shall we wear?' For the pagans run after all these things, and your heavenly Father knows that you need them. But seek first his kingdom and his righteousness, and all these things will be given to you as well. Therefore do not worry about tomorrow, for tomorrow will worry about itself. Each day has enough trouble of its own."

Matthew 6:31–34

The date I went withoug buying anything:

What difference did it make to the routines of my day?

What was the most awkward moment?

What I will remember between here and heaven:

67 Visit an ancient Christian site

How? A substantial list of ancient religious sites (mostly Christian, but some pre-Christian) can be found at www .sacredsites.com. Click "Americas" to find those that are in the United States. The majority are in the western half of the U.S. Spirit Mountain, near Laughlin, Nevada, glows bright red for two hours every morning that the weather is clear. In nearby Grapevine Canyon, ancient petroglyphs carved in the rocks portray the mythical history of the region.

Mauna Kea, the tallest volcano in Hawaii, shows evidence of glacial episodes that occurred more than 200,000 years ago. Moundsville, West Virginia, on the Ohio River, is the site of the Grave Creek Mound, an American Indian gravesite dating to 250–150 BC, the largest conical mound structure of its kind (69 feet high and 295 feet at the base).

Sacred sites are located all around the globe. Even if you can't visit most of them, they are all interesting to learn about. It is humbling to think about the places where past generations have worshiped and prayed.

What Should I Expect? The earliest Christian communities in Britain and Ireland were attracted to offshore islands and the edges of the land. There they could both retreat to be self-contained communities set apart for God, and also advance, using their home as a base from which to take the good news of Jesus from the fringes to the mainstream. Their isolation makes ancient Christian sites places of quiet serenity, and in the peace it is possible to experience a powerful sense of the Spirit of God making you one with those who shared your faith in centuries long gone. The ruins are sometimes just unexceptional stones, but they mark indelibly the presence of faith. You will realize that time has worn very thin the space between the sacred and the everyday.

Picture the Christians who first worshiped God in these places and recall their prayers that a nation which knew nothing of Jesus would be transformed by encountering him. Those prayers were answered in a way that exceeded anything they imagined. Even now, recognize that some Christians worship in small numbers on the edges of society, and let your hopes soar.

DON'T

Don't leave without adding to the prayers for the nation that have been said there for countless generations.

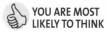 **YOU ARE MOST LIKELY TO THINK**

My brothers and sisters have kept the faith alive among these stones for hundreds of years, and I want to be as faithful as them in my generation.

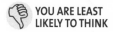 **YOU ARE LEAST LIKELY TO THINK**

Everything was easier for the Christians of previous centuries.

WHO SAYS?

Let your feet follow your heart until you find your place of resurrection.

Anonymous, possibly Columbanus, Irish monk and missionary, 540–615

To Help You Reflect

This is what the LORD says: "Stand at the crossroads and look; ask for the ancient paths, ask where the good way is, and walk in it, and you will find rest for your souls."

Jeremiah 6:16

Listen to me, you who pursue righteousness and who seek the LORD: Look to the rock from which you were cut and to the quarry from which you were hewn.

Isaiah 51:1

The date I visited an ancient Christian site:

Where? And what was there to see?

The impact it had on me:

What I will remember between here and heaven:

68 Read religious poetry

How? Buy or borrow an anthology such as *A Treasury of Christian Poetry* (edited by Mary Batchelor) or *The New Oxford Book of Christian Verse* (edited by Donald Davie). Do not attempt to read it from beginning to end, but drift around the book, allowing poems to catch your attention at random.

Then focus on particular poets. Some who are universally recognized as great writers wrote specifically to illuminate the Christian faith. Try the seventeenth-century poet John Donne (start with the defiant resurrection poem "Death Be Not Proud"), Gerard Manley Hopkins (a nineteenth-century Jesuit who composed the ecstatic praise of "God's Grandeur"), Emily Dickinson (an American poet of the nineteenth century whose short, simple verses, such as "The Only News I Know," glimpse heavenly truths), or the recent poet R. S. Thomas (a Welsh clergyman whose fiercely sublime poems, such as "The Coming," articulate this generation's faith which longs for assurance and wrestles with doubt).

What Should I Expect?

Ask yourself why the writer chose poetry, rather than prose, to say this about God. First of all, work out what the words actually mean. Then think about why he or she expressed them in that way. Are there rhymes and rhythms that suggest an orderly creation? Do the sounds of the words soar in a worshipful way, or grind to remind you of humankind's needs? How has the poet used the best words in the best order to give you an inspirational urge to engage with God?

When you read groups of poems by individual authors, try to work out what their unique style is, and what in God's nature they are inviting us to dwell on. Notice how the content of religious poetry has changed in passing centuries.

As you become more at ease with the attention that reading poetry requires, try some of the longer poems, becoming intrigued by the story they tell, being aware of the changing moods they create, and savoring the fact that every word was chosen by the poet in preference to a dozen alternatives. Let the ideas resonate with what you know of the Bible, of worship, and of life, and let phrases burrow into your memory to uplift you in subsequent days.

DON'T

Don't type "Christian poetry" into a search engine, because it will generate an avalanche of homespun verse that, although well-meaning, is sentimental and of a poor standard.

YOU ARE MOST LIKELY TO THINK

These words about God, honored by passing time, touch my soul because they are richer than anything I could have thought by myself.

YOU ARE LEAST LIKELY TO THINK

A poem isn't worth my time,
Unless the lines end with a rhyme,
And nothing useful rhymes with God,
But pod and cod and sod and odd.

To Help You Reflect

The Teacher searched to find just the right words, and what he wrote was upright and true. The words of the wise are like goads, their collected sayings like firmly embedded nails—given by one Shepherd.

Ecclesiastes 12:10–11

Pleasant words are a honeycomb, sweet to the soul and healing to the bones.

Proverbs 16:24

The date I read religious poetry:

Poets that made an impression on me:

A line that strikes me as beautiful and true:

What I will remember between here and heaven:

69 *Watch a different kind of movie*

How? If the films you usually see are in English, choose one that is in a foreign language and has subtitles. If they are usually made in Hollywood, choose one from Iran, Bollywood, France, or one of the other major centers of world cinema. If they are usually in color, watch a black-and-white film, or one from the era of silent movies. Or perhaps go to see a film in a genre that is new to you—for example, animation, science fiction, or documentary. Then try to put preconceptions out of your mind and surrender to the story.

To find a suitable film, read the reviews. Select a film in the knowledge that an expert thinks it has real worth, and watch it asking yourself why he or she saw virtue in it. Alternatively, go to a movie that has been chosen to be shown at a film festival, knowing that a panel has already selected it on its merits.

The Internet Movie Data Base (www.imdb.com) has the most extensive movie and TV listing in the world. You can read about almost any movie ever made, check on your favorite actor or director, and see what's in the works.

What Should I Expect? Enthusiasts of film, whether

or not they are looking at the movies from a Christian perspective, recognize cinemas as secular churches. Diverse people come together and have an experience that fills them with emotion and wonder, and makes them think deeply about the nature of the world they live in—some of the functions of a church service. Unlike churches, cinemas cannot build community, but by bringing people into the same room to have a shared and focused experience, a film can be as powerful spiritually as a service.

The reason for seeing a different kind of movie is that you will watch it with a different set of expectations. You will find yourself thinking about the predicaments of characters, rather than the performances of film stars. If you come out crying, what does the story tell you about God's activity in the world?

If it is a feel-good movie, what does the story strengthen you to do in order to make the world a place of hope? Instead of the fleeting fun of a typical evening at the cinema, ask yourself how the light that turned into images on the screen can enlighten you.

DON'T

Don't settle for second best by watching a DVD on television. See the film at its best, on a large screen, in the dark and with no distractions.

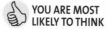 **YOU ARE MOST LIKELY TO THINK**

Because that film required more concentration than usual, I have had an experience that has more meaning.

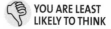 **YOU ARE LEAST LIKELY TO THINK**

The popcorn was more nourishing than the film.

WHO SAYS?

Film as dream, film as music. No art passes our conscience in the way film does, and goes directly to our feelings, deep down into the dark rooms of our souls.

Ingmar Bergman, Swedish stage and film writer, director

To Help You Reflect

Whatever is true, whatever is noble, whatever is right, whatever is pure, whatever is lovely, whatever is admirable—if anything is excellent or praiseworthy—think about such things.

Philippians 4:8

[God] has made everything beautiful in its time. He has also set eternity in the hearts of men; yet they cannot fathom what God has done from beginning to end. I know that there is nothing better for men than to be happy and do good while they live. That everyone may eat and drink, and find satisfaction in all his toil—this is the gift of God.

Ecclesiastes 3:11–13

The date I saw a different kind of film:

Its title:

In what way did it differ from the kinds of entertainment I usually choose?

What I will remember between here and heaven:

70 Invite your neighbors for a meal

How? For some people, inviting those who live on the same street into their homes is so natural that to give instructions for how to do it is insulting. Others struggle even to remember the names of people they see occasionally and wave to in the street. Having become neighbors, the sooner you offer hospitality, the easier it will be to do so. As time goes on, it becomes more difficult to knock on someone's door and invite them for a meal without giving the impression that you have a specific reason for doing so beyond simple neighborliness. If that is the case, take advantage of an occasion when circumstances bring you into conversation naturally.

Select food that allows you to give maximum attention to your guests and minimum attention to preparing the meal. Always choose something that you have cooked before (so that you are not anxious that it might go wrong) and something straightforward (so that your guests will not feel it would be burdensome to invite you back). Ask them in advance whether they have any particular dietary requirements. Do not stretch yourself beyond what you are confident to offer—a good experience of morning coffee and cake is better than an evening meal of three grim courses. Have in mind the first thing you will say to begin conversation, and then relax as you talk.

What Should I Expect?

Some people know so little about their neighbors that it is possible that Jesus Christ is alive in the house next door, and they are missing the opportunity to befriend him. Offering hospitality brings a new experience of God into your home, and having a meal together allows you to treat a neighbor as if you are serving Jesus.

Look for what is good and godly in the people. Ask questions that they will take pleasure in answering—about times when they have been happiest and places they have enjoyed. Listen to everything they say as if it matters a great deal, and remember it. You may be surprised to find that if you make a point of noticing the image of God in other people, they will glimpse the image of God in you without realizing it. You will have taken part in the most effortless and enjoyable evangelism, even though the name of Jesus may never be mentioned.

DON'T

Don't set out with the aim of suggesting that your neighbors come to a church activity. When your friendship has grown to the point at which they invite you to their favorite places, you will be in a comfortable position to invite them to come with you to church.

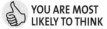 **YOU ARE MOST LIKELY TO THINK**

Somebody extravagantly and uniquely loved by God lives next door to me, and I hadn't realized it until today.

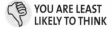 **YOU ARE LEAST LIKELY TO THINK**

I'm moving.

WHO SAYS?

Christians should offer their brethren simple and unpretentious hospitality.

Basil, bishop of Cappadocia (modern Turkey), 330–379

To Help You Reflect

Share with God's people who are in need. Practice hospitality. . . . Rejoice with those who rejoice; mourn with those who mourn. Live in harmony with one another.

Romans 12:13, 15–16

Keep on loving each other as brothers. Do not forget to entertain strangers, for by so doing some people have entertained angels without knowing it.

Hebrews 13:1–2

The date I invited my neighbors for a meal:

What we ate:

What we talked about:

What I will remember between here and heaven:

---

71 *Change the way you shop*

How? Altering the way you shop in order to improve the world involves a multitude of small changes. Buying fairly traded food is the simplest start, since most supermarkets stock a reasonable range. Fairly traded clothes, flowers, and footballs are harder to find, but progressively more visible. The Fairtrade Foundation publishes a list of stockists on its Web site (visit www .fairtradefederation.org, and click on "Find Members").

Organic food is also increasingly easy to find without changing the location in which you shop. However, there are good reasons to buy more local produce from independent shops and less food that has been flown wastefully around the world. The decisions are sometimes confusing. Eating a banana from the Caribbean makes a positive contribution to helping poor farmers, but buying foreign strawberries in January involves environmentally destructive freight and it is better to wait until summer when local ones are delicious. *The Rough Guide to Shopping with a Conscience* and the Web site www.ethicalconsumer.org help you make informed choices.

What Should I Expect? Whenever you get a bargain,

someone has subsidized it. Sometimes the shop's marketing strategy has paid for your good fortune, but more often it has passed the expense of your bargain on to a farmer in the developing world who earns pennies a day and is under pressure to drop his prices. Goods with the Fairtrade logo have been bought from a producer who has been guaranteed a minimum price, and there will also be an extra premium that is invested in the education or health of the community.

It is scandalous that as a result of the way we shop, mothers in the developing world are overcome by poverty and watch their children die of trivial diseases. When you buy fairly traded produce, or organic or local food that has not damaged the environment, you are making a statement that you believe other people's children deserve to thrive as much as your children. It demonstrates, in action rather than mere words, that you believe all people are loved and valued equally by God.

DON'T

Don't worry if you can't do everything at once. If you start with determination you will get an increasing taste for doing what is good until it becomes second nature.

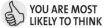 **YOU ARE MOST LIKELY TO THINK**

What's that strange, new flavor? Goodness!

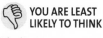 **YOU ARE LEAST LIKELY TO THINK**

I don't care.

Buy ethical! Buy fair trade! Buy organic! Buy local independent! Buy less! It really annoys me that the only way to get listened to is to spend money, but choosing who gets my money does make an eensy-weensy difference. And some suppliers are worth supporting and fairly traded coffee is actually very nice. That's why I do it. One person can't make a worldwide difference, but the alternative is not doing anything, and that's worse!

Laura Grimoldby, campaigner and commentator

To Help You Reflect

Hear this, you who trample the needy . . . skimping the measure, boosting the price and cheating with dishonest scales, buying the poor with silver and the needy for a pair of sandals, selling even the sweepings with the wheat. The LORD has sworn . . . "I will never forget anything they have done."

Amos 8:4–7

All a man's ways seem right to him, but the LORD weighs the heart. To do what is right and just is more acceptable to the LORD than sacrifice.

Proverbs 21:2–3

The date I changed the way I shop:

What I have stopped doing, and what I do instead:

What I have noticed about the quality:

What I will remember between here and heaven:

72 *Exercise*

How? Start by changing bad habits—use stairs instead of an elevator, walk to the corner shop instead of getting in a car, and adjust the television at the set instead of using the remote control. Then consider how you might improve your fitness by exercising regularly. The first choice is between taking up a competitive sport (such as joining a soccer or baseball team) or a fitness routine (such as swimming or aerobics).

To find a place where you can play a sport, contact your local park district or fitness center. Before beginning a regular sport or exercise, you should talk to your physician and have a basic checkup. Your physician can also help you locate a fitness program or sport that would be good for you. The Mayo Clinic Web site has helpful information on getting started with a fitness program: www.mayoclinic.com/health/fitness. If you have health issues, are pregnant, or haven't exercised regularly in a while, it is important to take these situations into consideration.

What Should I Expect? The writers of the New
Testament were concerned for the physical health of young Christians as well as their spirituality. John wrote that he was praying that Gaius would have a body as healthy as his soul. The Christian attitude was that the body was a "temple"—very different from the prevailing Greek attitude, which was that the body was an evil thing inside which a glorious soul was trapped. So getting fit is a way of honoring the body that God has given you. Exercise is more than just a leisure pursuit; it is a way that God has provided to make you comfortable inside your own skin. Regular exercise means that you will sleep better, feel less stress, and have fewer irritating aches and sniffles. As these things improve, you will find that you enjoy life more, and that is by far the best context in which to love and serve God.

DON'T

Don't exercise without consulting a doctor if you have any doubts about whether your health is suited to physical activity.

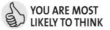 **YOU ARE MOST LIKELY TO THINK**

I'm not just fitter; I'm happier. That gives me even more reason to praise God.

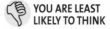 **YOU ARE LEAST LIKELY TO THINK**

I don't like feeling healthier.

WHO SAYS?

Swimming [is] my classroom where God teaches me so much about his ability, and [to have] faith in him. I love the sense of satisfaction that I get when I've done a swimming workout or race, and know that I gave my whole being and heart to God in every moment of the swim. It's the best worship I can offer him.
Penny Heyns, 1996 Olympic breaststroke gold medalist

To Help You Reflect

Do you not know that your body is a temple of the Holy Spirit, who is in you, whom you have received from God? You are not your own; you were bought at a price. Therefore honor God with your body.

1 Corinthians 6:19–20

Physical training is of some value, but godliness has value for all things, holding promise for both the present life and the life to come.

1 Timothy 4:8

The date I started to take exercise seriously:

What activity?

How I plan to make this a regular event:

What I will remember between here and heaven:

73 *Observe Ash Wednesday*

How? Ash Wednesday is the first day of Lent and it is observed forty-six days before Easter. Lent has historically been treated as a period in which to examine your life, be aware of behavior that is leading you away from God's standards, and make changes.

During many Ash Wednesday services, churchgoers have ashes smeared on their foreheads in the shape of a cross. This is a symbol of penitence and awareness of death. It is designed to be on display for the rest of the day, with Christians taking the sign of the cross into the world. The minister uses the words: "Remember you are dust, and to dust you shall return." Traditionally the ashes are made by burning palm leaves from the previous year.

Find the date of Ash Wednesday in the "Holidays by religion" section of www.earthcalendar.net. Contact local churches and find out the time of their Ash Wednesday services. Ask whether the service includes the imposition of ashes, since not all churches follow this ritual.

What Should I Expect?

The image of an ashen cross picks up many strands from the Bible. The most significant is the stories of creation that begin the Bible picture God forming Adam, the prototype human, from dust.

Without God, human beings would be nothing more than lifeless dust, and without the cross, humans would anticipate death as nothing more than disintegration. So the solemnity of Ash Wednesday is part of a cycle of sorrow and joy, failure and forgiveness, death and life, that makes up the experience of a believer and is reflected in the calendar of the Christian church.

If you continue to wear the ashes on your forehead during the day you will almost certainly catch the eye of passersby who will either be curious, be sarcastic, or assume that you are dirty. All those reactions are insignificant in comparison to the response of passersby to Jesus on his way to the cross, but they may help you recall what forgiveness has cost.

DON'T

Don't absentmindedly wash.

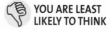 **YOU ARE MOST LIKELY TO THINK**

Why is everyone looking at me? Oh yes, I remember!

YOU ARE LEAST LIKELY TO THINK

Shall I take up smoking for Lent?

WHO SAYS?

We therefore commit this body to the ground; earth to earth, ashes to ashes, dust to dust; in sure and certain hope of the resurrection to eternal life, through our Lord Jesus Christ, who shall change our vile body, that it may be like unto his glorious body.

The Book of Common Prayer: interment prayers
from the service for the burial of the dead

To Help You Reflect

[God said to Adam:] "By the sweat of your brow you will eat your food until you return to the ground, since from it you were taken; for dust you are and to dust you will return."

Genesis 3:19

Repent, then, and turn to God, so that your sins may be wiped out [and] that times of refreshing may come from the LORD.

Acts 3:19

The date I observed Ash Wednesday:

The church where the ashes were imposed:

How I felt seeing my reflection in the mirror:

What I will remember between here and heaven:

74 *Go skinny-dipping*

How? There are a variety of places in the United States where skinny-dipping is encouraged. Descriptions and details of how to reach them can be found at www.swimmingholes.org, click "Skinny Dipping" under "National Water-Related Info."

There are, of course, many circumstances in which it is illegal to be naked in public—usually because the context suggests sexual aggression or is calculated to offend. Because of that, it is impossible for this book to recommend the romance and liberation of swimming nude at midnight in secluded waterfalls and remote lakes with the moon gleaming overhead. Oh well!

Choose a picturesque and isolated location. Make a base with your companions near the water. Line each other up, count down from ten, rip your clothes off, and sprint into the water. Have plenty of towels and thick clothes available, so that you can get dry and warm quickly when you emerge.

You should only skinny-dip with people with whom you know you are safe. Do not risk your own safety by going with people you do not know or don't particularly trust.

What Should I Expect? As you get over the cold

and start to enjoy the physical sensation, you will relax more and more about being undressed. The sense of daring that is common immediately before skinny-dipping gives way to a feeling of being embraced, enlivened, and at home in your own body. Most people find skinny-dipping a very pleasant sensation indeed, and it gives them an increased respect for the human body in which God has placed us. Your sense of self-worth will grow as you realize that in the water, without the clothes and accessories that give away everyone's status, you are all equally important and equally humble. This is how God sees you. To have thoughts like these at a moment when the physical sensation is so exhilarating is extremely uplifting. Reflecting on the event later, you may find yourself aware of the great dignity that God conferred on the human body by choosing to inhabit one when he was born as Jesus. That includes every kind of body—male and female, disabled or able-bodied, conventionally good-looking or not.

So you will become aware of your closeness to a loving God as you realize the goodness of being in God's image.

DON'T

Don't get arrested! And don't decide to do this under the influence of alcohol or any prescription or non-prescription drugs that may impair judgment, which increases the danger at the same time as it decreases the inhibitions.

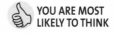 **YOU ARE MOST LIKELY TO THINK**

I'm glad I had a chance to do this!

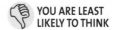 **YOU ARE LEAST LIKELY TO THINK**

I'm embarrassed that I did this.

To Help You Reflect

The LORD God caused the man to fall into a deep sleep; and while he was sleeping, he took one of the man's ribs and closed up the place with flesh. Then the LORD God made a woman from the rib he had taken out of the man, and he brought her to the man ... The man and his wife were both naked, and they felt no shame.

Genesis 2:21–25

You created my inmost being;
you knit me together in my mother's womb.
I praise you because I am fearfully and
   wonderfully made;
your works are wonderful, I know that full well.

Psalm 139:13–14

The date I went skinny dipping:

Which stretch of water?

Who was there and what made us decide to do it?

What I will remember between here and heaven:

75 *Visit an art gallery*

How? Visit www.usdirectory.com. Under "Business" enter "Art Gallery" plus your state or zip code to find an art gallery near you and its opening times. You do not need to book in advance; just show up. Go slowly, and afterward sit down in the café to think about what you have seen.

What Should I Expect?

There is no correct order in which to look at the paintings or sculptures. Drift from room to room, glancing at everything, but stopping and looking closely at works that seem interesting for any reason. In front of these, spend time making sure that you have examined every part of the piece.

Ask yourself: Is it a representation of something, or is it completely abstract? Is it telling a story or evoking a feeling? What can I see that I wouldn't be aware of if this were just a photograph? What is the mood of the piece, and how has the artist used color, shape, and composition to achieve that? Why did the artist choose this medium and this view?

After looking at the picture or sculpture (not before), read the label and find out the title, what it is made of, and when it was created. Sometimes there are also comments about the piece by an art expert. Having read them, look again at the artwork and ask yourself whether they have added to your understanding.

Next, look closely and work out how the artist made the piece. (Where did he use a thick brush and where a small one? How did he or she achieve the details? What tools were used to sculpt or construct?)

Finally, step back again and take in the work as a whole. What is its spiritual mood? Does it give off joy? Anger? Mystery? Pointlessness? Is it a religious piece (either portraying the Christian tradition or giving an insight into an aspect of what it means to be human)? Has it added anything to your inner world? If God had not invented words, might he communicate something through this?

Keep wandering, stopping at some pieces not just to see them, but to look at them. And at the end, reflect on which one you would take away with you if you were offered the choice. Buy a postcard of it in the shop before you go.

DON'T

Don't try to see everything in the gallery or you will get exhausted and stop enjoying it.

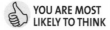 **YOU ARE MOST LIKELY TO THINK**

There are some thoughts that can't be expressed in a sentence. Maybe God can tell me something through my eyes and feelings that I would never understand through words.

 **YOU ARE LEAST LIKELY TO THINK**

I could have done that. (If you do think it, the fact is that you didn't do it, did you!)

WHO SAYS?

Art washes the dust of everyday life from your soul.
—*Pablo Picasso, artist, 1881–1973*

To Help You Reflect

The LORD has chosen Bezalel son of Uri . . . and he has filled him with the Spirit of God, with skill, ability and knowledge in all kinds of crafts—to make artistic designs for work in gold, silver and bronze, to cut and set stones, to work in wood and to engage in all kinds of artistic craftsmanship.

Exodus 35:30–33

Since the creation of the world God's invisible qualities—his eternal power and divine nature—have been clearly seen, being understood from what has been made.

Romans 1:20

The date I visited an art gallery:

Where?

Which works of art made an impact on me?

What I will remember between here and heaven:

76 *Fast for a day*

How? If you have never fasted before, attempt a 24-hour fast from lunch to lunch (missing two meals). During that time eat no food, but drink plenty of water, and perhaps fruit juice. If your family circumstances permit it, pray or read the Bible during meal times. As you notice physical sensations that you are not used to, remind yourself that you are doing this as a sign between you and God that this is a special occasion. Use it to ask him to direct you. Pray, confess, or be thankful for something significant. Be aware of the injustice of the world that leaves millions permanently hungry. You will feel best if you end your fast by eating salad, fruit, and bread, rather than a heavy meal.

What Should I Expect? To begin with you will find the physical aspects of what you are doing interesting, but try to monitor your inner attitudes as well, and be aware of what God brings into your mind. Fasting is not magical, and certainly not a way of twisting God's arm. It is, however, a way of prioritizing things that need your attention, knowing that they are already of great concern to God.

You will probably feel hungry at some points. This is not real hunger, however. It is your body responding to the fact that you have conditioned it to expect to receive food at certain points during each day. If you decide not to eat at that point, it is a way of expressing your willingness to let God be in control of your life. Every mundane activity of your normal day is being done with this act of worship going on as its backdrop.

You will find yourself relating the fast to other areas of your life about which you are not content (from irritations on a bus journey to major concerns about relationships). Ask God to help you sort the trivial from the vital, and open yourself to his guidance. You will also be aware of the difference between your desire for food and the very different predicament of those who are hungry because of poverty. This too will make you reconsider your priorities, and may result in decisions that will change you. In all these cases, God will be revealing to you, body and soul, what it means to surrender yourself to God.

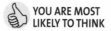 **YOU ARE MOST LIKELY TO THINK**

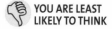 **YOU ARE LEAST LIKELY TO THINK**

DON'T

Don't fast if you are pregnant, diabetic, or receiving treatment for a heart condition. If you are in any doubt as to whether this would injure your health, ask your doctor. Don't embarrass friends by turning up to a dinner party and announcing that you won't eat. And don't stuff yourself with food before or after the fast, because that defeats the purpose.

God is my absolute priority at this moment, and the physical feelings inside me keep reminding me that there is a great deal that I need to sort out with God.

The thing the world needs most is more fast-food outlets.

WHO SAYS?

What the eyes are for the outer world, a fast is for the inner world.
Mahatma Gandhi, Indian statesman, 1869–1948

To Help You Reflect

"You eat, but never have enough. You drink, but never have your fill. You put on clothes, but are not warm. You earn wages, only to put them in a purse with holes in it." This is what the Lord Almighty says: "Give careful thought to your ways."
Haggai 1:6–7

"When you fast, do not look somber as the hypocrites do, for they disfigure their faces to show men they are fasting. I tell you the truth, they have received their reward in full. But when you fast, put oil on your head and wash your face, so that it will not be obvious to men that you are fasting, but only to your Father, who is unseen; and your Father, who sees what is done in secret, will reward you."
Matthew 6:16–18

The date on which I fasted:

What I did with the time when I would usually be eating:

Adjectives that describe my feelings at various stages:

What I will remember between here and heaven:

77 *Send a virtual gift*

How? Charity Navigator (www.charitynavigator.org) is an online organization that evaluates the financial health and integrity of more than 5,000 of the largest charities in the United States. It not only provides information about specific charities, but answers many questions about charities in general. You can browse charities by category and even make direct donations to the charities of your choice through a secure online service, "Network for Good." Many charities will send a gift card on behalf of the giver, if you choose to make a donation as a gift or to honor someone through your giving.

Some charities, such as Heifer International (www.heifer.org), even have a gift registry. To celebrate a special occasion such as a birthday, wedding, or holiday, you can put together a wish list of charitable gifts that friends and family can give in your honor to others in need. In this way, you can make a difference in the world, cut back on unnecessary consumerism, and avoid a cluttered closet full of items you will never use.

What Should I Expect? An operation to restore the
sight of a blind person in India costs about the same as giving someone a pair of designer pants. Almost anyone can appreciate which of those has a more lasting value. The joy of a virtual gift is that it shows someone you love that you thought specifically of them and imaginatively matched them up with an appropriate present. They feel appreciated, you know that you haven't been trapped into wasting money by the commercialism of Christmas, and someone in the developing world will have their life transformed.

Sending a virtual gift is one of the few ways of giving to charity that guarantees cheerfulness, and because the Bible tells us that God loves a cheerful giver, we know that even God shares in the rejoicing. Giving generously to needy people reflects the actions of Jesus, who gave himself to be born in great humility instead of in a palace.

DON'T Don't give a virtual present to someone who might mistakenly interpret your great concern for the world's poorest people as a sign that you don't care for them sufficiently to buy a more usual gift.

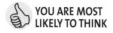 **YOU ARE MOST LIKELY TO THINK**

These are the most worthwhile presents I have ever purchased.

YOU ARE LEAST LIKELY TO THINK

I should have bought something for myself instead.

To Help You Reflect

Each man should give what he has decided in his heart to give, not reluctantly or under compulsion, for God loves a cheerful giver. And God is able to make all grace abound to you, so that in all things at all times, having all that you need, you will abound in every good work. As it is written: "He has scattered abroad his gifts to the poor; his righteousness endures forever."

2 Corinthians 9:7–9

One man gives freely, yet gains even more; another withholds unduly, but comes to poverty. A generous man will prosper; he who refreshes others will himself be refreshed.

Proverbs 11:24–25

The date I sent a virtual gift:

What and to whom?

In which country will people benefit from what I have done?

What I will remember between here and heaven:

78 *Run a foot race*

How? A good list of marathons, half-marathons, and other races can be found at www.runnersworld.com/cda/racefinder. You may be able to register online for a race in your area, or at a destination to which you would like to travel. It is up to you to find the discipline to keep to an arduous training schedule over several months. The race information might suggest ways of using the run to generate money for charity.

Most races require you to register in person the day before, where you collect a race number, a kit bag, and a computerized chip to attach to your shoe, which will record your precise time. At the finish, expect a medal, a T-shirt, a massage, and a feeling of exhilaration!

If at any point in the race, you can't breathe or your body tells you to "stop!" then "stop!" Although it isn't surprising to feel like stopping during a marathon, know your limits. You are not a failure if you don't finish.

What Should I Expect?

One of the reasons that foot races are popular is that, although they are extremely daunting, they are not impossible. Ordinary people, if they are single-minded, can achieve something extraordinary. The training (a combination of short jogs, increasingly long runs, and rest) is extremely good for your body. The race, while grueling for your body, is extremely good for your sense of worth. No one will take the achievement from you. And using the race to raise money for charity ensures that your pride in the success is shared generously. In perseverance, joy, and pain, it is a model for the whole of a worthwhile Christian life.

DON'T

Don't set off so fast that you have to give up (either the training or the event). Like life itself, finishing matters.

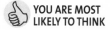 **YOU ARE MOST LIKELY TO THINK**

Having achieved something extremely difficult with God's help, I can look at other difficult things in my life in a more positive way.

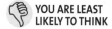 **YOU ARE LEAST LIKELY TO THINK**

I think I'll do that again tomorrow.

WHO SAYS?

Training for and running the marathon is like having a chance to survey the course of your Christian life—the decision to begin, the challenge to stick with the programme, the victories, the set-backs, the desire to quit conflicting with the desire to endure and reach the ultimate goal. It teaches you that nothing is really achieved without effort. A marathon is completed one step at a time.

James Smith, participant in the Cincinnati "Flying Pig" marathon

To Help You Reflect

Do you not know that in a race all the runners run, but only one gets the prize? Run in such a way as to get the prize. Everyone who competes in the games goes into strict training. They do it to get a crown that will not last; but we do it to get a crown that will last forever.

1 Corinthians 9:24–25

The date I ran a race:

In which city?

My finishing time:

What I will remember between here and heaven:

79 *Investigate a saint*

How? Access a biographical dictionary of saints (hagiography). Many books delineate the lives of saints, both well known and not. Visit the Web site www.catholic.org and click the link to "Saints and Angels" for quick access.

Choose to investigate a saint whose name you have heard of— perhaps because his image appears on a stained glass window, a local church is dedicated to her, or because you share a name or a date of birth. Then let your curiosity lead you from saint to saint.

What Should I Expect? In the Bible, the word "saint" is used simply to mean a faithful Christian. The word means "holy," and can apply to believers who are living or dead. However, the common use of the word is to describe someone from the past whose life was righteous and inspirational. In some traditions there is a process involving research and prayer over many years by which particular people come to be recognized officially as saints (canonization).

Saints are examples to the Christian community of how we should all behave. Their stories are passed on over the years (sometimes retold with such relish that the actual truth of their lives is less interesting than the embellishments) so that future generations will be encouraged and have their faith in God made strong.

Read the story of saints' lives fully aware that the legend may have outgrown the truth, but attempt to understand what virtue there was in the men, women, or children that inspired people to want to honor them by preserving the story. What was it about their faith in Jesus Christ that allowed them to achieve more than seems possible to most Christians? What would that kind of devotion look like in a Christian who is alive in this generation? What would you be doing now if you had that kind of character? What's stopping you?

DON'T

Don't be anxious about traditions that involve praying to saints. The inspiration you get from the life of a saint may help you pray, so make the most of that, but it cannot make a prayer better or worse. God's response will be perfect, and nothing about your prayer can make him more perfect than perfect!

WHO SAYS?

Saints are people who make it easier for others to believe in God.

*Nathan Söderblom,
archbishop of Uppsala,
1866–1931*

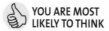 **YOU ARE MOST
LIKELY TO THINK**

This was an ordinary Christian person who did ordinary Christian things, but he or she did them very much better than others, and with selfless motives.

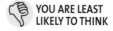 **YOU ARE LEAST
LIKELY TO THINK**

I'll be on that list one day.

To Help You Reflect

Remember your leaders, who spoke the word of God to you. Consider the outcome of their way of life and imitate their faith.

Hebrews 13:7

Some faced jeers and flogging, while still others were chained and put in prison . . . destitute, persecuted and mistreated—the world was not worthy of them. They wandered in deserts and mountains, and in caves and holes in the ground. These were all commended for their faith, yet none of them received what had been promised. God had planned something better for us so that only together with us would they be made perfect.

Hebrews 11:36–40

The date I investigated the life of a saint:

The name of the saint:

The most interesting thing about his or her life:

What I will remember between here and heaven:

8O *Help promote literacy*

How? Even in a country with as many resources as the United States, millions of people don't know how to read or write, or need help with math skills, written tests, learning disabilities, and other literacy issues.

If you can read this book, you can help.

The National Institute for Literacy and Partners sponsors a Web site, America's Literacy Directory (ALD): www.literacydirectory.org. This site is designed for people who need assistance with reading, writing, basic math, or studying for the GED or other high school equivalency tests, or who are more comfortable with a language other than English. Links connect you to agencies in your area where you can receive assistance, and to ways that you can volunteer as a tutor, teacher, teacher's aide, or student volunteer, or help with administrative duties. The toll-free telephone number is 1-888-228-8813.

Consider starting a group at your church where volunteers come in on an afternoon, evening, or weekend to read to children, or go to the homes of older adults and others who would love to have someone come and read to them. Your library may have programs for reading and delivering books to the homebound. There are many ways that you can encourage reading, writing, and arithmetic, for all ages.

Many churches and agencies now have a child protection policy in place. This may require you to have a background check if you are working with children. Don't be offended if you are asked to provide permission for a background check. This is not done out of suspicion about you, but solely for the welfare of the youngest members of society.

What Should I Expect? You will be pleasantly surprised at what you can do, and you'll feel good knowing that you are helping people develop skills that will benefit them in more ways than you will ever know. As you meet people one on one or in a group, you'll quickly move beyond any stereotypes you've had tucked away in your mind.

The people to whom you give your time may do the same for someone else down the road. You are part of a chain of events with far-reaching consequences.

DON'T

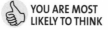 **YOU ARE MOST LIKELY TO THINK**

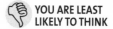 **YOU ARE LEAST LIKELY TO THINK**

Don't be judgmental. Keep an open mind, and be glad you can do something for those who may not have had the educational opportunities that you have had.

I wish I'd thought of doing this before. What a great use of my time!

It's boring to read aloud to someone else.

WHO SAYS?

Once you learn to read, you will be forever free.

Frederick Douglass, abolitionist, reformer,
statesman, author

To Help You Reflect

For wisdom will enter your heart, and knowledge will be pleasant to your soul.

Proverbs 2:10

Whatever you do, whether in word or deed, do it all in the name of the Lord Jesus, giving thanks to God the Father through him.

Colossians 3:17

The date I contacted a literacy agency:

The specific way in which I volunteered:

How I plan to continue working for literacy:

What I will remember between here and heaven:

81 Pray in an airport chapel

How? Large airports, and some smaller ones, have a chapel. Often the room is a space for prayer shared by several faiths. The pattern across the world varies (widespread in the United States, but rare in Australia). Even in places where there is no chapel, airports tend to have a chaplain. Check online before you travel and see if a particular airport has a chapel, and where it is.

Airport chapels tend to be plain, comfortable, and sensitively lit. Most are open and untended from morning to evening, and have a notice giving the times of occasional services and details of how to contact the chaplain. They can be used for personal prayer, but chaplains will pray with groups before they travel together or with individuals. In many airports, Christian staff meet for prayer and fellowship. On the rare occasions when airports become gathering places following an accident, chaplains are key to the pastoral care.

What Should I Expect? Airport terminals are large

and disorienting places. They have the features of shopping centers, with attention-grabbing displays. Airport chapels are designed to contrast completely. They are uncluttered, relaxing, and built on a human scale. They are kept simple so that everyone can share them. Most do not have religious symbols in recognition that airports are gathering points for people of all the world's religions. It is acceptable for Christians to bring their own symbols with them.

Moving from the commotion of a terminal into the quiet of a chapel unveils an airport's best-kept secret. Before traveling at great speed, slow down to a point at which you are very still. In this place through which people of every nationality pass, take the opportunity to think about what it means to be in the care of the God who is creator of the heavens as well as the earth, and of every religion of humankind as well as the Christians. If you are nervous about flying, use the tranquillity to commit the journey to God, knowing that God will accompany you through the turbulence in as real a way as God is with you in the calm.

DON'T

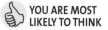 **YOU ARE MOST LIKELY TO THINK**

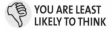 **YOU ARE LEAST LIKELY TO THINK**

Don't underestimate how long it will take to reach your plane.

In this bustling place I have momentarily slowed down to a pace at which I can meet God, and now I am conscious that God's blessing will be with me above the clouds.

What they most need here is another outlet for cheap booze and jewelry.

WHO SAYS?

I see myself as the last outpost of unashamed Anglican ministry.... For passengers frightened to fly, refugees, those meeting and greeting, stressed-out staff from the police, airlines and hotels, I keep the faith flying.

David Smith,
former chaplain
to Heathrow Airport

To Help You Reflect

Where can I go from your Spirit?
Where can I flee from your presence?
If I go up to the heavens, you are there;
if I make my bed in the depths, you are there.
If I rise on the wings of the dawn,
if I settle on the far side of the sea,
even there your hand will guide me,
your right hand will hold me fast.

Psalm 139:7–10

Great is your love, higher than the heavens;
your faithfulness reaches to the skies.
Be exalted, O God, above the heavens,
and let your glory be over all the earth.

Psalm 108:4–5

The date I prayed in an airport:

The name of the airport and my destination:

I prayed about:

What I will remember between here and heaven:

82 Read the Bible from cover to cover

How? The most straightforward way to read the Bible is to start at the first book, Genesis, and read a chapter every day. There are, however, disadvantages to reading the Bible in this way. The later books speak to the spirit of a Christian in a much more vital way than those at the start, but it will take two and a half years to reach the part about the life of Jesus! And the Bible books are ordered in a way that keeps the various genres (prophecy, letters, laws, and so on) together, which does not lend itself to variety if you are reading from beginning to end.

There are several alternative ways of reading the whole Bible, most of which involve reading about three chapters daily. It is possible to follow a plan that allows you to read the Bible in chronological order, so that the unfolding story of God's dealings with humankind becomes clear. Or you can read it in the order in which the books may have been written. Other plans allow you to read part of the Old Testament and part of the New Testament every day, sometimes yielding unexpected insights and comparisons. You can find reading plans at www.backtothebible. org. Click on "Bible Studies and Devotions" and then "Bible Reading Guides." There are options for historical, chronological, and straight-through reading plans. If you don't like one, choose another.

What Should I Expect?

When you read the entire Bible, it becomes less likely that a single sentence or issue from it will dominate the way you view your faith, and more likely that you will become engrossed by the vast scale of the project on which God is working.

With each chapter, ask yourself what kind of literature you are reading. Is it someone's life story? (How is their life an example of faith?) Is it advice given to an ancient people about how to be godly? (If so, what would be the equivalent advice to today's world?) Is it poetic language? (Does this speak to your heart?)

Some things you will find shocking. Let them anger you! Some things you will find inspiring. Enjoy the exhilaration! Do not be dispirited by things you cannot understand, but keep reading so that the overall themes of the Bible—love, justice, faith—are the ones that leave their mark on you.

DON'T

Don't give up in the middle of Numbers.

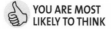 **YOU ARE MOST LIKELY TO THINK**

The words are ancient, but some of them take on startling new significance in the light of events in the twenty-first century.

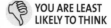 **YOU ARE LEAST LIKELY TO THINK**

The sequel is not as good as the first one.

WHO SAYS?

Most people are bothered by those passages of Scripture they do not understand. But the parts that bother me are the ones I do understand.

Mark Twain, writer, 1835–1910

To Help You Reflect

All Scripture is God-breathed and is useful for teaching, rebuking, correcting and training in righteousness, so that the man of God may be thoroughly equipped for every good work.

2 Timothy 3:16–17

Everything that was written in the past was written to teach us, so that through endurance and the encouragement of the Scriptures we might have hope.

Romans 15:4

The dates when I began and ended my reading of the Bible:

The parts I enjoyed most and least:

My feelings at having completed it:

What I will remember between here and heaven:

8**3** *Make a sharing arrangement*

How? Begin by identifying things that you need to use only occasionally—say, every six months. Among these might be a power drill, a vacuum for autumn leaves, or a kitchen implement that does a very specific job. Put a message in your church newsletter explaining that you own these items and are investigating whether anyone would like to share them, or that you intend to buy something and wonder whether one or two people would like to share the ownership and the cost. If people respond, meet with them and discuss where the objects will be located and how you can be sure you can all have access to them when they are needed. Record on a piece of paper what it is you are sharing and the addresses and phone numbers of all the people involved. Although it is not necessary to sign this as a formal agreement, discuss what will happen when someone moves or no longer wants to be part of the agreement, and make a note of it. And then decide together what to do with the money you have saved. Set it free to be used to do good.

If this proves a success, consider making a similar arrangement for things you use more frequently, bearing in mind that you need to live closer to someone. Work on the possibility of making a genuine impact for environmental good by sharing a car, a washing machine, or something else in daily use.

What Should I Expect? The object of making
a sharing agreement is that the good you achieve together outweighs the inconvenience of not having something in your possession every moment of every day. The good includes money released for good causes, and the benefit to the environment of less waste, but also the trust and cooperation that builds friendships.

In the church in Jerusalem during the years after Jesus' resurrection, the way Christians shared their property and lives was so marked that need came to an end in the community. It made such an impression on those who watched it happening that it drew them to faith. Making a sharing arrangement goes so completely against today's culture that it will make as deep an impression on people now as then, so don't be shy about letting people know about it!

DON'T

Don't lose track of the agreement you have made, so that you make sure there can never be bad feeling because one of you forgets what you arranged.

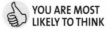 **YOU ARE MOST LIKELY TO THINK**

Sharing has given me deeper friendships as well as saving me money.

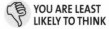 **YOU ARE LEAST LIKELY TO THINK**

But I can't possibly manage without a wallpaper stripper of my own.

To Help You Reflect

Command [those who are well off] to do good, to be rich in good deeds, and to be generous and willing to share. In this way they will lay up treasure for themselves as a firm foundation for the coming age, so that they may take hold of the life that is truly life.

1 Timothy 6:18–19

All the believers were one in heart and mind. No one claimed that any of his possessions was his own, but they shared everything they had. With great power the apostles continued to testify to the resurrection of the Lord Jesus, and much grace was upon them all. There were no needy persons among them.

Acts 4:32–34

The date I set up a sharing arrangement:

What and with whom?

The advantages and disadvantages so far:

What I will remember between here and heaven:

84 Visit a nursing home

How? Because elderly and sick people are vulnerable, there are safeguards to ensure that visiting a nursing home is a positive experience for everyone concerned. It is not possible to knock unannounced on the front door and ask for immediate access to visit strangers. Ask the leaders of your church whether they have a relationship with residences in the area where you might visit.

If the church does not have a pastoral plan of this kind, contact a nursing home and ask whether they would welcome a regular visitor to talk with the residents. If you have special skills, such as hand massage, beauty treatment, music, or leading exercise or worship, explain what you could offer. But initially these are less significant than a willingness to sit and chat. Be ready to make an appointment to speak to the manager and prove your identity. Explain how much time you could offer, and be prepared to fit in with what is needed, rather than imposing your own ideas in an insensitive way.

Make a contact through someone you know who has a family member or friend in a nursing home. Perhaps there is a roommate who never gets a visit with whom you can visit. Make sure with the staff that you are not invading someone's privacy by making a visit. Some families might not appreciate your good intentions.

What Should I Expect?

Most nursing homes warmly welcome regular visitors, because their staff are overstretched by attending to the physical needs of their clients. Some residents have no visitors at all, and a new friendship gives them emotional support, a rhythm to their week, and a sense of dignity.

Playing board games or sharing crafts (chess or knitting, perhaps) may give a starting point, but also begin conversations about memories and experiences. And if the person has a disability that makes talking difficult, being present in silence is valuable of itself. Remember continuously that the image of God is present in each person and seek it out. What do wrinkles tell you about God's nature? Or deafness? Or gentleness? Or loneliness? You are that next generation! Expect to learn the power of God through your visits.

DON'T

Don't begin a friendship with someone and then stop visiting unexpectedly or on whim. Only make commitments that you know you can fulfill.

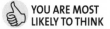 **YOU ARE MOST LIKELY TO THINK**

There is a deep wealth of experience and wisdom within the walls of nursing homes, and it is foolishness to waste it.

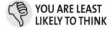 **YOU ARE LEAST LIKELY TO THINK**

Poor old soul!

 WHO SAYS?

A society which treasures the elderly and disabled, and looks after them, is a generous society. Once this stops, life becomes cheap.
Basil Hume, Roman Catholic archbishop, 1923–1999

To Help You Reflect

"I was hungry and you gave me something to eat, I was thirsty and you gave me something to drink, I was a stranger and you invited me in, I needed clothes and you clothed me, I was sick and you looked after me, I was in prison and you came to visit me. . . . I tell you the truth, whatever you did for one of the least of these brothers of mine, you did for me."

Matthew 25:35–36, 40

Religion that God our Father accepts as pure and faultless is this: to look after orphans and widows in their distress and to keep oneself from being polluted by the world.

James 1:27

The date I began to visit a nursing home:

The names of the people I talked to:

Something interesting from one of my conversations:

What I will remember between here and heaven:

85 *Collect for a charity*

How? Few people enjoy getting lots of requests for donations in the mail or over the phone, even when the charities asking for help are ones whose work we believe in and wish to support. Yet the hard truth is that most charities depend on bringing their needs to our constant attention in order to raise the funds that are needed for research and support services.

Charity Navigator (www.charitynavigator.org) is a great place to start if you want to learn more about a charity that has approached you for help or if you want to decide which charities you want to support. You can discover the percentage spent by reputable charities on fundraising. And you can help cut back on administrative costs by volunteering to help make phone calls or gather collections in your neighborhood. Check the charity's Web site (links are provided at Charity Navigator) for contact information.

If you agree to make a neighborhood collection, you will be sent a list of addresses and phone numbers (when provided) for a section of your neighborhood. You will receive envelopes to leave with your neighbors, and you will be asked to provide postage for their return to you. Once all donations are collected, you send the total to the charity in one envelope, thus cutting additional postage costs.

What Should I Expect?
Collecting for a charity is humbling. Our experience of someone asking us for money is usually limited to a destitute person begging, so when you collect for a charity you show yourself willing to identify with that helplessness. You risk rejection and insult—it is not a pleasant thing to do. It would be easier simply to write a check.

However, knocking on doors and making people aware of a pressing need is an act of witness. Its impact goes far beyond the usefulness of the money that is collected, because it announces the values of the kingdom of God to the neighborhood. It reminds them that poor people need good news, suffering people need rescue, and unhappy people need peace. This was the work of Jesus, who was humbled to the point of wretchedness, and this is a way of coming alongside him in sacrificial service.

DON'T

Don't let a shower
of rain daunt
you—people are more
generous to a collector
who perseveres in
adverse conditions.

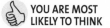 **YOU ARE MOST
LIKELY TO THINK**

That was tough, but not
nearly as tough as the
circumstances suffered
by the people on whose
behalf I was collecting.

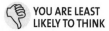 **YOU ARE LEAST
LIKELY TO THINK**

I have collected enough.

WHO SAYS?

Christ has no body now
on earth but yours, no
hands but yours, no feet
but yours. Yours are the
eyes through which
Christ's compassion for
the world is to look out;
yours are the feet with
which he is to go about
doing good; yours are
the hands with which
he is to bless.

*Teresa of Avila, abbess and
mystic, 1515–1582*

To Help You Reflect

[Jesus said,] "Be careful not to do your 'acts of righteousness' before others,
to be seen by them . . . When you give to the needy, do not announce it
with trumpets, as the hypocrites do in the synagogues and on the streets,
to be honored by others. . . . Do not let your left hand know what your right
hand is doing, so that your giving may be in secret."

Matthew 6:1–4

The date I collected money for charity:

Where?

How much did you collect and for which charity?

What I will remember between here and heaven:

86 *Pray in a cathedral*

How? The largest cathedral in the world is the Cathedral of St. John the Divine in New York City. A list of all the cathedrals in the United States can be found at http://en.wikipedia.org/wiki/List_of_cathedrals_in_the_United_States. From there, you can click on your state and find the names and locations of cathedrals of various denominations. Most cathedrals are open to the public during a good portion of the day, but call before you visit to be sure that the building will not be closed for a special event.

There are three ways of praying in a cathedral. Attend a service led by the resident choir, or a shorter spoken service, or use the cathedral at any time for personal prayer. A choral service feels in some ways like an exceptional performance, with the congregation encouraged to join in a few items. A spoken service has a smaller scale, with a greater emphasis on praying for the world. Personal prayer allows you to meet God in a place where many have prayed before you, and the lofty setting gives this a unique feel.

What Should I Expect?

The scale of the building makes praying in a cathedral unique and, no matter what kind of prayer you engage in, the space has an impact. At a choral service, the magnificent acoustics give the sound of the choir an ethereal quality that will lead you to reflect on the grandeur and holiness of God. The formality of the occasion reflects a desire that everything offered to God in worship over the centuries (the building itself and everything that takes place within) should have an enduring excellence, because that is what God deserves.

As you take part in spoken or silent prayer, the space around you will take on a sense of enveloping godliness, and the echoes will intensify your awareness of the God who listens attentively. Be conscious of the thousands who have prayed in this place before you and (if it is a historic building) the sense of awe and delight that Christians of previous centuries, unused to tall buildings, had as they walked the same paving slabs.

DON'T

Don't run out of patience with tourists who come and go as you pray. They too have been drawn to the cathedral to experience something out of the ordinary, and that is a response to their spirituality, even if they do not recognize it. If they distract you, pray for them.

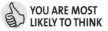 **YOU ARE MOST LIKELY TO THINK**

The Christian faith has a past, a present, and a future in this land.

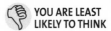 **YOU ARE LEAST LIKELY TO THINK**

I can't wait to get back out into the traffic.

To Help You Reflect

How lovely is your dwelling place, O LORD Almighty!
My soul yearns, even faints, for the courts of the
    LORD;
my heart and my flesh cry out for the living
    God. . . .
Blessed are those who dwell in your house;
they are ever praising you.

Psalm 84:1–2, 4

The date I prayed in a cathedral:

Which one?

What I prayed about:

What I will remember between here and heaven:

87 Make a confession

How? In the Roman Catholic tradition, priests make themselves available during the hour before mass to hear people confess what they have done wrong. A structure like a large cupboard with two doors allows you to talk to a priest confidentially through a grille. You will be aware of his presence, but not threatened by it. He will ask what you want to confess (there is a traditional form of words, but a sensitive priest will help you if you do not know how to express yourself). He will suggest what you might do to repair the damage you have done to another person, and what prayers you might say to restore your relationship with God. He will then assure you of God's forgiveness with a sentence of which the crucial words are, "I absolve you."

In Protestant traditions, a church leader will listen to you confess sins whose shame you want to be rid of. Some churches do this in a formal way. In other churches there will be more informality, but all will end with an assurance that you are forgiven, and pastoral advice.

There are circumstances in which confessing to a trusted Christian friend, who understands your circumstances, is more directly helpful. There are also Internet sites such as www.dailyconfession.com, on which it is possible to write anonymously.

What Should I Expect?

Doing wrong impedes your ability to live your life to the fullest, with joyful and peaceful relationships. But God is able to forgive sins so completely that they lose their power to spoil relationships. Forgiveness requires an acknowledgment of the damage you have done, a genuine regret, and a sincere intention not to offend again.

All Christian traditions recognize that only God can forgive sins, so it is to God that you make your confession. However, it is difficult to express your thoughts honestly to God, and revealing the truth to another person and hearing them say, "God forgives," is extremely liberating. Depending on how heavily the burden of having done wrong weighs on you, you may feel relief instantly. But equally you may feel few emotions, and only discover as days go by that you are able to view people you have wronged in a different way.

WHO SAYS?

Since the communion of last Easter I have led a life so dissipated and useless, and my terrors and perplexities have so much increased, that I am under great depression and discouragement. Yet I purpose to present myself before God tomorrow, with humble hope that he will not break the bruised reed.

Samuel Johnson, writer, 1709–1784

 DON'T

Don't allow confession to grow so routine that the experience becomes trite. It is too important.

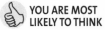 **YOU ARE MOST LIKELY TO THINK**

I have taken responsibility for my own actions, and glimpsed myself as God sees me. There is now nothing to stop me putting the past behind me and becoming the person I want to be.

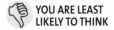 **YOU ARE LEAST LIKELY TO THINK**

I got off lightly!

To Help You Reflect

If we claim to be without sin, we deceive ourselves and the truth is not in us. If we confess our sins, he is faithful and just and will forgive us our sins and purify us from all unrighteousness.

1 John 1:8–10

Day and night your hand was heavy upon me;
my strength was sapped as in the heat of summer.
Then I acknowledged my sin to you
and did not cover up my iniquity.
I said, "I will confess my transgressions to the LORD"—
and you forgave the guilt of my sin.
Therefore let everyone who is godly
pray to you while you may be found.

Psalm 32:4–6

The date I confessed a sin that had previously been a secret:

To whom?

How I felt before and after:

What I will remember between here and heaven:

88 *Learn the Seven Wonders of the Ancient World*

How? Can you name the Seven Wonders of the ancient world? Good for you if you can. If you can't, now is the time to learn.

The naming of the Seven Wonders dates back to BC times. A Greek writer named Philo, from the city of Byzantium, compiled the traditional list in 225 BC in *On the Seven Wonders*. The Greek word for "wonders" actually can be translated as "must-sees." Many of the "must-sees" are tributes to Greek culture (only two of the original Seven Wonders were not Greek).

The seven: the Great Pyramid of Giza, the hanging gardens of Babylon, the statue of Zeus at Olympia, the temple of Artemis at Ephesus, the mausoleum of Maussollos at Halicarnassus, the Colossus of Rhodes, the lighthouse of Alexandria. Of these seven, only one is still standing. Do you know which one it is?

Encyclopedias and online resources list the Seven Wonders and tell you what you need to know. Perhaps the more vital question here is, why learn about structures that have long since been destroyed?

We learn from the past. We come to a greater understanding of the dominance of various cultures and how these cultures have shaped the world we live in. We can appreciate the architectural and construction skills of people who lived long before modern conveniences. We gain insight into what other peoples have considered to be of importance and worth.

For a quick and insightful virtual tour, check out CNN's travel Web site: http://www.cnn.com/TRAVEL/DESTINATIONS/9705/seven.wonders.

What Should I Expect?
As you study the Seven Wonders of the ancient world as well as the wonders of various ages and cultures, keep this in mind: the greatest wonder of the world is the world itself! Nobody can re-create a mountain, an ocean, a desert, the skies, a sunset. The wonder of God's creation certainly tops anything ever made by humankind. Expect a renewed sense of wonder in all that God formed out of the chaos, in the very beginning of time.

DON'T Fascinated? Then don't stop at learning the wonders of the ancient world. There are lists of the wonders of the medieval world, the wonders of the modern world, the wonders of the industrial world, the wonders of the underwater world, and the new Seven Wonders of the ancient world, not to mention the additions to the original list.

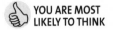 **YOU ARE MOST LIKELY TO THINK**

How did they do that without the modern tools we have now?

YOU ARE LEAST LIKELY TO THINK

That looks easy. I think I can turn my patio in another hanging gardens of Babylon.

To Help You Reflect

I will remember the deeds of the Lord; yes, I will remember your miracles of long ago. I will meditate on all your works and consider all your mighty deeds. Your ways, O God, are holy.

Psalm 77:11–13

The date I memorized the Seven Wonders:

The wonder that most interests me:

What I consider a must-see in the world:

What I will remember between here and heaven:

89 Imagine yourself into a bible story

How? Choose a single event from one of the narrative sections of the Bible. You are going to imagine yourself to be a witness to it, so select one in which many people were observing—possibly a resurrection appearance of Jesus, the occasion of a miracle, or an episode from the trek of the Hebrews through the wilderness. Read and familiarize yourself with the story.

Then shut your eyes and, in your imagination, see what is happening as if you were one of the people involved in it. Enter the story as an active participant, but one with an incidental part to play. Feel the sand beneath your sandals, smell the sea, hear the conversation, sense the sun on your head, taste the food. Let the story unfold in your mind. Work out the emotions that are being experienced by the people involved. If characters speak to you, give an appropriate answer. If they come toward you, move in response.

Be particularly aware of how you react to Jesus or to the main characters. After several minutes, imagine yourself leaving the scene and walking away, then walk yourself back into the reality of the twenty-first century. Ask yourself what you noticed that you had not been aware of before.

This visualization of Bible stories was a style of meditation advocated by Ignatius of Loyola, the founder of the Society of Jesus (Jesuits), who lived in the sixteenth century.

What Should I Expect?
To start with, you will find yourself an observer, seeing the stories at a distance, like a film. However, as you get used to contemplating stories in this way, it becomes more natural to place yourself in the thick of events, becoming part of the action.

There is no need to try to analyze the event intellectually or gather insights to share with others. Instead, apprehend it through your sense of smell, taste, and other feelings, so that you are more intrigued by its reality than its meaning. Ask questions of the characters, and find out what they say to you as the written word of the Bible becomes a living presence.

Think afterward about what difference it would make if the presence of Jesus, saying and doing the things you have just imagined, was a reality.

DON'T

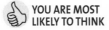 **YOU ARE MOST LIKELY TO THINK**

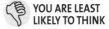 **YOU ARE LEAST LIKELY TO THINK**

Don't change the ending of the story, even if you can think of a better conclusion, or allow those in your retelling of the story to do something out of character.

Some lucky people really did get close enough to Jesus to brush against his cloak and hear his stomach rumble.

Those Bible dudes had it cushy!

To Help You Reflect

The word of God is living and active. Sharper than any double edged sword, it penetrates even to dividing soul and spirit, joints and marrow; it judges the thoughts and attitudes of the heart.

Hebrews 4:12

Jesus told [Thomas], "Because you have seen me, you have believed; blessed are those who have not seen and yet have believed."

John 20:29

The date I imagined myself into a Bible story:

The story I meditated on:

Things I noticed about the story for the first time:

What I will remember between here and heaven:

90 *Discover Celtic Christianity*

How? Church leaders met at Whitby in 664 to seek God's will about the future of Christianity in Britain. They chose to follow the way the faith was practiced in mainland Europe. But before Augustine arrived from Rome to convert England, Jesus had been worshiped on these islands for many years following the practices of missionaries who had come from Ireland via Scotland and northeast England.

In recent decades this Celtic form of Christianity has been rediscovered, because many issues that were important to the believers of the time have emerged again—for instance, the need to protect the earth, and the place of women in God's plan. There are many Web sites devoted to Celtic Christianity, and www.celticchristianity.org links to interesting articles. A visit to the offshore islands that were centers of Celtic Christianity, Lindisfarne and Iona, enables you to understand the context in which these traditions first thrived.

What Should I Expect?

Celtic Christianity is shaped by a love of nature and by appreciation of art and music, all of which are a gift of God. There is no distinction between sacred and secular. Every aspect of work and play is full of potential to be a way of learning from and serving God.

Celtic Christians saw their life as a pilgrimage and had a vivid sense of the unseen presence of God and Christians who had gone before them. They recognized God in every aspect of creation and human creativity, so their prayers were both earthy and poetic. There was time for contemplation as well as time for energetically making Jesus known. They cared for the environment and were passionate to improve the lot of the world's vulnerable, poor, and sick people. It came naturally to them to respect women's leadership as well as men's. No wonder their way of life has inspired today's Christians to apply their wisdom to this generation.

DON'T

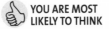 **YOU ARE MOST LIKELY TO THINK**

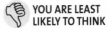 **YOU ARE LEAST LIKELY TO THINK**

Don't think that the Celts lived only in Ireland.

My faith is worthless if it does not have an impact on every aspect of the way I live on this planet.

The experience of Christians who lived hundreds of years ago can't teach anything to this technological age.

WHO SAYS?

[For Celtic Christians] the natural landscape was both a concrete reality where people lived and a doorway into another, spiritual world. The sense of living in a "between place" enabled Celtic Christians to make connections between . . . the seen and the unseen, this world and a permanently present "other" world.

Philip Sheldrake, theologian

To Help You Reflect

Let the word of Christ dwell in you richly as you teach and admonish one another with all wisdom, and as you sing psalms, hymns and spiritual songs with gratitude in your hearts to God. And whatever you do, whether in word or deed, do it all in the name of the Lord Jesus, giving thanks to God the Father through him.

Colossians 3:16–17

The date I found out about Celtic Christianity:

The most interesting discovery:

Elements that I could incorporate into my own life:

What I will remember between here and heaven:

91 *Take part in a Passover meal*

How? For thousands of years the Jewish people have celebrated the Passover (or Seder) to commemorate their release from slavery in Egypt. It is at once a family meal, a history lesson, and an act of worship. It was this supper that Jesus ate with his followers the night before he died, and Christians remember it through Communion.

Jewish Lights Publishing (www.Jewishlights.com) offers several good books explaining the meaning and rituals of the Seder. There are also instructions, recipes, and reflections from a Christian perspective at www.christianseder.com, which has links to the words that are said in the liturgical part of the event (the *haggadah*) that are adapted in the light of Christian theology.

Invite guests of all ages and set the table for dinner. Add a bowl of salt water, parsley sprigs, three *matzah* (brittle, flat bread), *charoset* (puréed nuts, fruit, and wine), horseradish, a hard-boiled egg, a shank of lamb, a candle, wine glasses, and one more seat than the number you are expecting. Each person needs a copy of the *haggadah*, because there are words that everyone says together during the story of how God rescued his people many centuries ago and still upholds them lovingly today. The elements on the table are used to bring the story to life, and in the middle of the prayers and readings, the meal is served.

What Should I Expect? Sharing a Passover meal
not only brings to life the roots of the faith in Judaism, it can also give a new richness to your appreciation of the Christian act of worship.

Every element of the ritual means something. The salt water recalls the tears of the Hebrews in slavery, the lamb calls to mind the animal that was sacrificed on the eve of their departure from Egypt, the bread is unleavened to recall the haste at which they left, the egg is a symbol of new life, and so on. The empty chair is traditionally left for Elijah, the great prophet of justice and hope.

Christians can bring their own symbolism to the traditions, for instance, seeing the Trinity in the three *matzah*, one of which Jesus described as his own body when he broke it in the presence of his followers. The wine toasts life, freedom, reconciliation, and an end to oppression—the very things for which Jesus went to the cross.

DON'T

Don't skimp on the meal. You are worshiping God as much by eating as by praying.

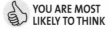 **YOU ARE MOST LIKELY TO THINK**

This is the meal that Jesus ate in sadness and fear so that I can eat it today in joy and thankfulness.

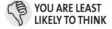 **YOU ARE LEAST LIKELY TO THINK**

Worship only counts when it's boring.

To Help You Reflect

[Jesus] said to [his followers], "I have eagerly desired to eat this Passover with you before I suffer. For I tell you, I will not eat it again until it finds fulfillment in the kingdom of God."

Luke 22:15–16

Christ, our Passover lamb, has been sacrificed. Therefore let us keep the Festival, not with the old yeast, the yeast of malice and wickedness, but with bread without yeast, the bread of sincerity and truth.

1 Corinthians 5:7–8

The date I took part in a Passover meal:

With whom?

The things I ate and drank:

What I will remember between here and heaven:

92 *Write a prayer*

How? Clarify the kind of prayer you are writing. It might be a prayer that simply tells God that you worship and revere him because of his nature; one that thanks God for something; one that asks for forgiveness for wrong things you (or your entire society) have done; or one that asks God to act in response to a need. Jot a few words down about the subject to act as notes.

First, decide how to address God. For instance, if it is a prayer for forgiveness you might say "Merciful Lord" or another title that focuses on God's compassion; a thankful prayer could begin, "Generous God." Then write what you want to say to God in straightforward words. There is no need to attempt phrases that sound clever, lofty, or biblical. However, to write a prayer rather than improvise it gives you the chance to use words that are not simply chatty. As a guideline, use the kinds of words you would use in a letter. However, split up the sentences into phrases of eight to ten words, starting each on a new line at natural breaks, such as commas or new ideas.

End your prayer with the phrase "Through Jesus Christ our Lord," or simply, "Amen."

What Should I Expect?
There are two advantages to a prayer that you write—you can keep it, and you can share it. Keeping it means that in days (or even years) to come you can look back and recall the concerns that were important to bring before God at a particular time. This helps you become continuously aware of how God is responding to your prayers, either by changing you or by changing the world.

Sharing your prayer can happen when it is read aloud in the context of a church service, or simply when you show a friend what you are praying. For a church service, if you are leading prayers of intercession, read through what you have written and ask yourself whether it is something with which everyone in the congregation will be able to agree. Your task is to give them words that encourage them to take the needs of the world to the heart of God, so try to be engaging and create positive phrases that inspire people. The same is true of other ways in which you can share your prayer—on Web sites, in church magazines, or by e-mail to your friends.

DON'T

Don't imagine that God is impressed by the quality of the writing—only by the sincerity of the prayer.

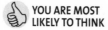 **YOU ARE MOST LIKELY TO THINK**

The extra thought that went into this prayer has helped me speak clearly to God, but it has also helped me listen to God.

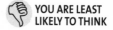 **YOU ARE LEAST LIKELY TO THINK**

Now God will do just what I tell him to do.

To Help You Reflect

I urge, then, first of all, that requests, prayers, intercession and thanksgiving be made for everyone—for kings and all those in authority, that we may live peaceful and quiet lives in all godliness and holiness. This is good, and pleases God our Savior.

1 Timothy 2:1–3

I will pray with my spirit, but I will also pray with my mind.

1 Corinthians 14:15

The date I wrote a prayer:

The subject:

The context in which I shared or prayed it:

What I will remember between here and heaven:

185

93 *Explore religions you know little about*

How? The Religion Facts Web site (www.religionfacts.com) presents information about thirty world religions, including Buddhism, Sikhism, and Hinduism, in an objective way. (It stretches the definition of religion to include sects.) The major religions are described over many pages, covering their history, worship, and scriptures. However, there are also concise résumés, with charts comparing facts and statistics.

A variety of books describe the history and beliefs of the religions of the world. But don't limit your exploration to Web sites and books. Visit museums that display art and artifacts from around the world. Find out about a religion that is less well known than the major ones. Investigate the presence of places of worship in your area.

Suggest that your church hold a series of classes on world religions. Bring in experts who also practice different avenues of faith. Come with an open mind and an attitude that allows discussion and differences of opinion.

What Should I Expect? Researching religions

through books is engrossing, but merely knowing the facts does not give you a sense of the hope, healing, and love that those who practice them find. Your discoveries will be greatly enhanced when you befriend someone whose life is shaped by worshiping and obeying God through adherence to their religion.

All religions are seeking answers to the same fundamental questions: How have we come to be here? What is the purpose of human life? What is our destination when our bodies wear out? Expect to encounter people who have set their hearts on doing good and are looking for strength through their faith in God to fulfill their lives and improve the world, now and eternally. As you discover this, the trivia about those who practice other religions (such as their dress and unfamiliar rituals) will become less significant than admiration for their desire to live in a way that pleases God.

DON'T

Don't imagine that you can understand a religion by knowing all the facts about it. Only those who have said "yes" to a belief system know it fully.

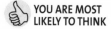 **YOU ARE MOST LIKELY TO THINK**

No matter how big any religion is, God is bigger.

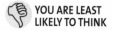 **YOU ARE LEAST LIKELY TO THINK**

All religions are the same—just with different names for God.

WHO SAYS?

The uniqueness of Christianity is in Jesus Christ. He is the stumbling block of all ideologies and religious systems. . . . [He] deserves to be the goal and standard for individuals and humankind. . . . I consider traditional religions, Islam and the other religious systems to be preparatory and even essential ground in the search for the Ultimate. But only Christianity has the terrible responsibility of pointing the way to that ultimate Identity, Foundation and Source of security.

John Mbiti, Kenyan theologian

To Help You Reflect

But if from there you seek the LORD your God, you will find him if you look for him with all your heart and with all your soul.

Deuteronomy 4:29

The date I explored other religions:

Something new I discovered:

Something that has given me hope:

What I will remember between here and heaven:

94 *Find out what you are worth*

How? Visit the Global Rich List at www.globalrichlist.com. Enter your annual salary in U.S. dollars. A graph will then reveal where you fit on a scale between the richest and poorest people of the world. Using information from the World Bank's development research group, the Web site will calculate the number of people in the world who are poorer than you, and tell you the percentage of the world's richest people to which you belong.

What Should I Expect? It comes as a shock to

almost everyone that their income, no matter how modest, is very substantial indeed compared with the vast majority of the world. Halving or even quartering your income, which would dramatically change your way of life, makes virtually no difference to your place on the scale between the world's richest and poorest people.

Further research reveals greater ironies. The world's 225 richest people have a combined wealth that is the equivalent of the world's poorest 2.5 billion people. In 1820 the richest 20 per cent of the world's population received three times as much as the poorest 20 per cent. By 1960 it had escalated to a scandalous 30 times. In 2002, the richest received 114 times as much as the poorest.

The challenge that comes with knowing your true worth is to use the information in a worthwhile way. Logic would suggest that realizing you are among the very richest people of the world should lead to a deep content and generosity. However, experience shows that the sentiment most likely to be generated by wealth is a desire for slightly more wealth.

The way of Jesus is to be content no matter the circumstances in which you find yourself. He challenged his followers to measure their commitment to the kingdom of God by selling everything and giving the proceeds to the poor. Ask yourself what you would have to do if you discovered tomorrow that you had $1,000 per year less. And then $5,000 per year less. Expect God to put in your mind actions you could take in order to make the gulf between your way of life and that of someone living in poverty slightly less extreme.

DON'T

Don't use this as an excuse for a spending spree.

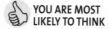

YOU ARE MOST LIKELY TO THINK

I had no idea that the little I have is so much in comparison with others.

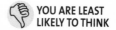

YOU ARE LEAST LIKELY TO THINK

I deserve to be in this place on the scale between the richest and the poorest.

To Help You Reflect

Our desire is not that others might be relieved while you are hard pressed, but that there might be equality. At the present time your plenty will supply what they need, so that in turn their plenty will supply what you need. Then there will be equality, as it is written: "He who gathered much did not have too much, and he who gathered little did not have too little."

2 Corinthians 8:13–15

I ask of you, O Lord . . . Give me neither poverty nor riches, but give me only my daily bread. Otherwise, I may have too much and disown you and say, "Who is the Lord?" Or I may become poor and steal, and so dishonor the name of my God.

Proverbs 30:7–9

The date I found out my financial worth:

Exactly how many of the world's people are poorer than me?

The changes I will make as a result of what I have discovered:

What I will remember between here and heaven:

95 *Watch an eclipse of the sun*

How? A total solar eclipse can be seen when the moon, on its orbit around the earth, comes between you and the sun. A dark, curving shadow appears to eat into the sun, giving it a crescent shape, then covering it completely, like a black disc surrounded by a ring of light. Day turns briefly to night as the moon's shadow falls on you. The temperature drops and birds begin to sing because they think it is dusk.

Total eclipses of the sun are rare and only visible from certain places on the earth's surface on any occasion. On July 22, 2009, it will be possible to see an eclipse in India, Nepal, and China. On January 15, 2010, the eclipse can be seen in Central Africa, India, and China. The next will be on July 11, 2010, visible in the south Pacific, Chile, Argentina, and Easter Island, and on November 13, 2012, in northern Australia. For more information on the solar eclipse, go to www.happynews.com/living/space/solar-eclipse -viewing.htm.

What Should I Expect? Ancient literature describes eclipses, but without understanding their cause. They are described as fearful events, associated with vengeful gods demanding that people change their wicked behavior. The Old Testament anticipates the "great and dreadful day of the Lord," which will bring about the destruction of God's enemies and the deliverance of his followers, taking place during an eclipse.

For those who observe an eclipse during this century, the wonder is equally great, even though the reason is known and the date foreseen. Why? Perhaps because it reminds us of the complexity of the universe that God has placed us in, about which we know so much and yet so little, and which is so orderly and yet constantly unpredictable.

DON'T Don't look directly at the sun. If you do, the lens of your eye will act like a magnifying glass and burn a hole in the retina. The safest method to view an eclipse is to make a pinhole in a sheet of paper and allow it to cast the sun's image on a screen. Despite rumors, watching through smoked glass or exposed camera film is extremely dangerous. Filters made from aluminized mylar are sold in optical devices made specially for viewing the sun. The only part of an eclipse that is safe to look at with the naked eye is the few spectacular seconds of total darkness.

YOU ARE MOST LIKELY TO THINK

This is an awesome moment, and reminds me that it was God who first drew light out of darkness.

YOU ARE LEAST LIKELY TO THINK

The gods are angry with us.

WHO SAYS?

No. It made me feel really, really small.
Neil Armstrong, the first human to walk on the surface of the moon. Noticing that he could blot out the Earth with his thumb, he was asked, "Did that make you feel really big?"

To Help You Reflect

The day of the LORD is near in the valley of
     decision.
The sun and moon will be darkened,
and the stars no longer shine.
The LORD will roar from Zion
and thunder from Jerusalem;
the earth and the sky will tremble.
But the LORD will be a refuge for his people,
a stronghold for the people of Israel.

Joel 3:14–16

The date, time, and place I saw an eclipse of the sun:

A sequence of drawings of what I saw:

My emotions:

What I will remember between here and heaven:

96 *Dance in the rain*

How? No amount of planning will prepare you for this moment. One unusually warm summer evening, at the end of a long dry period, the rain will tumble and this will prove irresistible. It is unlikely that you will be alone (although no one should rule it out); it is more likely that you will be with friends who share faith and trust. As the climax of a conversation or activity that makes you feel glad to be alive, open the door of the house or leap out of the car and start jumping around. You don't need music or any kind of technique—just excitement. A shower, a hot drink, and a change of clothes will protect you against any subsequent feeling of regret!

What Should I Expect? The legacy of the Puritans is that most people picture the Christian faith as requiring restraint and sacrifice. This, however, is only part of the story. There is an element of Christian experience that can only be expressed through spontaneity and exuberance. Spontaneity was a feature of Jesus' life (for which Zacchaeus will be eternally grateful) and so was exuberance (defending himself for feasting with Matthew when others thought he should be fasting). Jesus knew the moment for solitude and the moment for gaiety. In his letters to the churches in the years after Jesus' resurrection, Paul urges them on nine occasions to overflow—with joy, thankfulness, love and hope.

The recklessness of dancing in the rain for the sheer joy of being alive is a reflection of the recklessness of God in creating a world teeming with color and variety, and then entrusting it to mere human beings. It will remind you why, on the verge of his death, Jesus prayed for his followers to have joy, not to have dignity. No matter what age you are, after doing this you will be younger!

DON'T

Don't overdo it and wake up with a cold. And don't get this book wet!

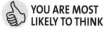 **YOU ARE MOST LIKELY TO THINK**

I'm singing in the rain, just singing in the rain. What a glorious feeling; I'm happy again!

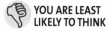 **YOU ARE LEAST LIKELY TO THINK**

Slow, slow, quick, quick, slow!

WHO SAYS?

There was taken away from men all fear of those who had formerly oppressed them. They celebrated brilliant festivals. All things were filled with light, and men formerly downcast looked at each other with smiling faces and beaming eyes. With dancing and hymns in city and country alike they gave honor first of all to God the King of the universe.

Eusebius of Caesarea, historian of the early years of the Christian church, writing about the victory of Emperor Constantine, 260–330

To Help You Reflect

David, wearing a linen ephod, danced before the LORD with all his might, while he and the entire house of Israel brought up the ark of the LORD with shouts and the sound of trumpets.

2 Samuel 6:14–15

The date I danced in the rain:

Where?

What made me so joyful that I did it?

What I will remember between here and heaven:

97 *Make your own Christmas cards*

How? Organize yourself at the end of November, deciding on a design and buying the materials you need. The simplest way to personalize Christmas cards is to choose a photograph of your family or a winter scene, have copies made and paste them to the front of a folded card. Create your own message and print it using a word processing package or write it if you have fine handwriting.

The links at www.makingcards.com offer many designs and suggestions, as well as advice and online shops. There is, however, no substitute for your imagination, which allows you to create a design that expresses what Christmas means to you.

Rubber stamps and ink pads are another popular way to make your own cards. While purchasing numerous supplies can be expensive, a fun way to make this cost effective is to have a stamping party with friends who own stamps. Make several batches of cards to sell at a craft fair, and give the money to a charity of your choice. If you really want to make it a party with meaning, arrange to bring supplies to a nursing home or shelter, and invite the residents to make cards to give to their loved ones or friends.

What Should I Expect?

The salvation of the world could not be bought; it could only be given. That is the meaning of Christmas. God invested everything of himself in the creation of Jesus, and in doing so took an incalculable risk in order to demonstrate the extent of his love. During the Christmas season, every time you make something instead of buying it, you share in a small way in the creativity of God that brought about the first Christmas.

In an age that values time more than money, making your own Christmas cards is a demonstration of the extent of care you have for your friends and family. It allows you to choose images and write words that express your own feelings about God taking human, vulnerable flesh, instead of settling for someone else's clichés. And the process slows you down sufficiently to think about and pray for each person for whom you make a card.

DON'T

Don't be overanxious about professionalism, because the charm of a homemade Christmas card lies in its wobbly edges.

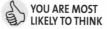 **YOU ARE MOST LIKELY TO THINK**

This year I gave people time and care, instead of money.

 **YOU ARE LEAST LIKELY TO THINK**

My Christmas has just been a commercialized sham.

To Help You Reflect

Finish the arrangements for the generous gift you had promised. Then it will be ready as a generous gift, not as one grudgingly given.... Each man should give what he has decided in his heart to give, not reluctantly or under compulsion, for God loves a cheerful giver.

2 Corinthians 9:5, 7

Give, and it will be given to you. A good measure, pressed down, shaken together and running over, will be poured into your lap. For with the measure you use, it will be measured to you.

Luke 6:38

The date I made Christmas cards:

What was the design? (Draw a miniature version):

The number I made and sent:

What I will remember between here and heaven:

98 *Hug someone*

How? The most common hugs take place between two people in an upright position. Beginners will require the following technical information:

The "greeting hug" is the most familiar. Both huggers extend their arms at right angles to their bodies. They step forward and place their arms around each other's torso.

The "comfort hug" is used to bring solace to someone close to you in a time of need, and ministers at a depth that words cannot match. It is especially effective between parents and children.

The "shoulder hug," usually reserved for lovers, has the arms encircling the neck instead of the back, thus locating the huggers' hearts in close proximity. Prior permission is vital for this intimate hug, which might otherwise be mistaken for attempted strangulation.

The "seated hug" should only be attempted by agile people, since it involves the spine twisting in an unnatural way. More comfortable is the "reverse hug." The hugger approaches from behind and passes his or her hands around the huggee's waist. The element of surprise adds to the delight of this most affectionate of hugs, best reserved for those who share a long-established affection.

Multiperson variations include the "sandwich hug," for three people of differing heights (often two parents and a child), in which the central person has the experience of being enveloped in fondness. The "group hug" is formed by a circle of people with their arms around each other's waists. When performed by a sports team or at a party it expresses celebration and mutual joy.

Always be respectful of a person who would rather not be hugged, and don't make a big scene if someone declines the offer of a hug.

What Should I Expect?

A good hug, generously offered and willingly received, is one of the most underrated experiences of life. It doesn't harm the environment, contains no calories, and leaves you feeling better both physically and spiritually. Treat it as paradigm of God's unmerited grace. (Oh, forget that! Just enjoy it!)

DON'T

Don't indulge in the "unwanted hug," in which a hugger persists despite the reluctance of the other person. This is abusive and recognizable by the unwilling party twisting her hip and tipping her head backward. And don't cause jealousy by leaving certain people unhugged.

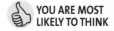 **YOU ARE MOST LIKELY TO THINK**

What a great invention.

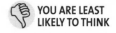 **YOU ARE LEAST LIKELY TO THINK**

Hugs are for others, not me.

WHO SAYS?

I will not play at tug o'war,
I'd rather play at hug o'war,
Where everyone hugs instead of tugs,
Where everyone giggles and rolls on the rug,
Where everyone kisses, and everyone grins,
And everyone cuddles, and everyone wins.
Shel Silverstein, children's poet, 1930–1999

To Help You Reflect

[There is] a time to weep and a time to laugh,
a time to mourn and a time to dance,
a time to scatter stones and a time to gather them,
a time to embrace and a time to refrain.

Ecclesiastes 3:4–5

The date I gave a memorable hug:

Who?

What was the occasion?

What I will remember between here and heaven:

99 *Plan your funeral*

How? Write a letter expressing things that are important to you about the way your life should be celebrated. In it, answer these questions: Where would you like the funeral to take place? Would you prefer to be buried or cremated? Do you want your organs made available for transplant? Is there anyone whom you would like to take part in the service? What mood should it have? What music would you appreciate being played? What Bible passages or poems could be read? Is there a symbol or action that would make the occasion unique? Would you like flowers, or would you prefer donations to be made to a charity—if so, which one? Do you have any requests about a lasting memorial?

Place these instructions with your will. Decide who you would like to take responsibility for the arrangements, and tell that person where they will be able to find the letter when the time comes. Think about who you would like to come to your funeral, and create a list of names and contact details so that the person arranging it does not miss anyone who should be informed.

What Should I Expect? This is partly a gift to

yourself and partly a gift to the people you love. For you, it is an opportunity to work out what has been most significant in your personality or achievements, and to think of ways in which that can be expressed through music, words, or actions. It is also a chance to witness to what God has meant to you during your life, and the hope you have about spending eternity with him. For your family and friends, who will be experiencing sadness or shock in the days after your death, it provides reassurance that they are doing something that would give you pleasure. Expect this to be a life-affirming exercise, making you even more appreciative of the people, words, and music that God has given to enrich your life so far.

DON'T

Don't use your funeral as an opportunity to settle old scores or send hidden messages. Sort those things out while you are alive.

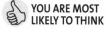 **YOU ARE MOST LIKELY TO THINK**

This will help the people I love to remember me with pleasure as well as with grief.

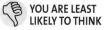 **YOU ARE LEAST LIKELY TO THINK**

I hope I make people cry.

WHO SAYS?

It's good to have to think about death. Death's what's real in life. It's just that we find ways to be busy. If we lived every day with death, we would live a different life and it would not necessarily be a depressing one. It would probably be more joyful. You know, I often lose the ability to prioritize. I'm rushing to get lunch for the children, and put the toilet paper on the toilet paper thing, and read the scripts, and it takes a kid getting sick or something to remember that it's not so important that there's stuff all over the floor and maybe, just maybe, you should play with your kids. People say that if we think about death all the time we'd go mad, but maybe we'd go sane.   *Susan Sarandon, actress*

To Help You Reflect

"Death has been swallowed up in victory."
"Where, O death, is your victory?
Where, O death, is your sting?"
1 Corinthians 15:54b–55

The date I planned my funeral:

The place where I left instructions:

The part of my life for which I am most grateful:

What I will remember between here and heaven: